D1456349

Presented to

_____

By

_____

Date

_____

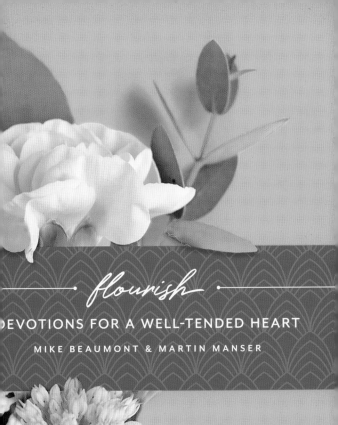

flourish

DEVOTIONS FOR A WELL-TENDED HEART

MIKE BEAUMONT & MARTIN MANSER

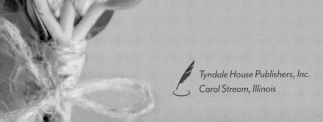

Tyndale House Publishers, Inc.
Carol Stream, Illinois

LIVING
EXPRESSIONS
COLLECTION

Living Expressions invites you to explore
God's Word in a way that is refreshing to
the spirit and restorative to the soul.

Visit Tyndale online at www.tyndale.com.

TYNDALE, Tyndale's quill logo, *Living Expressions*, and the Living Expressions logo
are registered trademarks of Tyndale House Publishers, Inc.

Flourish: Devotions for a Well-Tended Heart

Designed by Jennifer Ghionzoli

For information about special discounts for bulk purchases, please contact Tyndale
House Publishers at csresponse@tyndale.com, or call 1-800-323-9400.

ISBN 978-1-4964-4125-6

Printed in China

26   25   24   23   22   21   20
7   6   5   4   3   2   1

The godly flourish like leaves in spring.

PROVERBS 11:28

Contents

New Beginnings

Anyone who belongs to Christ has become a new person.
The old life is gone; a new life has begun! 2 CORINTHIANS 5:17

THERE ARE FEW who aren't moved by a newborn baby. Perhaps it's their freshness, or helplessness, or the fact that everything seems so perfect. Little wonder they can make us think, *If only I could make a brand-new start!*

At such times we need to remember the Bible's promise that we can—because when we trust in Jesus, the old life really has gone, and a whole new life begins!

So here you are, beginning this book of devotions and perhaps longing for a new beginning in your relationship with God. Such beginnings can't happen by self-effort or self-improvement, but only with the Holy Spirit's help (Romans 8:26).

If you haven't yet been "born again" (John 3:3), today is a good day to ask Jesus to bring that about. But if you have, remember that you can keep enjoying this new birth by constantly being "filled with the Holy Spirit" (Ephesians 5:18).

And remember, too, that even if you've made a mess out of your life or find yourself in a dry place, God can always give you a fresh start—again! Don't listen to the devil's accusations or his lies—listen instead to the promises of God's Word.

Resolve to let a song of worship well up within you today as you take hold of this new beginning with your Lord. With him, what has been does not need to shape what will be! Believe that today.

The one sitting on the throne said,

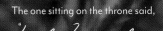

"Look, I am making everything new!"

REVELATION 21:5

MAIDEN PINK

Dainty, fringed maiden pink
flowers create a beautiful
ground cover that deer don't
bother but bees and butterflies
love. They're native to Asia
and Europe.

Who is Eternal

All honor and glory to God forever and ever! He is the eternal King, the unseen one who never dies; he alone is God. Amen. | 1 TIMOTHY 1:17

HAVE YOU EVER BEEN CONFUSED by all those dates stamped on food in stores? "SELL BY . . ."; "USE BY . . ."; "DISPLAY UNTIL . . ."; "BEST BEFORE . . ."—phrases designed to give you the freshest of food, but oh-so-confusing at times. Or have you witnessed seeing the latest technology sitting alongside the heavily discounted previous model, now so clearly out of date? What a fast-changing world we live in!

In light of this, it's incredibly reassuring to remember that our God is "the LORD, the Eternal God" (Genesis 21:33). In other words, he has no "SELL BY" or "BEST BEFORE" date; there is no new model due out soon that will replace him. He is eternal! This not only means he is without beginning and without end—for that in itself might be rather boring—but also that he is unchanging and unchangeable, yet at the same time always up to date and ever new.

And because God is eternal, he shows eternal love (1 Kings 10:9), gives eternal blessings (Psalm 21:6), offers eternal life (John 3:16), and rules an eternal kingdom (Daniel 4:3). Yes, everything about him is eternal. Remembering this makes such a difference in life.

Today, don't be small minded or short term in your thinking. Your God is eternal—and so are his purposes for you. Thank him for that and ask him to take you further along the path of those eternal plans.

The eternal God is your refuge, and his everlasting arms are under you. DEUTERONOMY 33:27

CHRYSANTHEMUM

...ysanthemums, or mums, are ...nature flower of autumn and ...ve to Asia. Swedish naturalist ...rolus Linnaeus, the father of ...taxonomy, named them.

Knowing Christ

I want to know Christ and experience the mighty power that raised him from the dead. PHILIPPIANS 3:10

WE ALL HAVE DEEP LONGINGS, some of them known only to ourselves. Paul's deepest longing was known by everyone: It was simply to know Christ. Yet didn't he already know him? Oh yes! But his desire was to know him better and better, even (especially!) when life wasn't going well.

When Paul wrote Philippians 3:10, he wasn't participating in a joyful worship service or a happy midweek group with friends; no, he was in jail. Most of us would have wanted to escape so we could get on with life, but Paul stayed right where he was, confident that Christ was there with him. In fact, wherever Paul was, he knew that Christ was always present, so he simply kept focusing on his Lord.

The trouble for many of us is that our spiritual perception quickly gets blurred when the kids start acting up, or the cake gets burned in the oven, or the car won't start, or the money won't stretch. But that's when we simply need to *stop*—and activities such as personal daily devotions and weekly corporate worship force us to do that. They give us a clear vision of Christ once again so we can press on to knowing him better and trusting him more.

Don't settle for anything less than his presence, right where you are. Whatever you are facing, it can't be worse than suffering in prison for your faith! Reset your focus on Christ, for it is only in knowing him that we can also experience the power of his resurrection.

Some Greeks who had come to Jerusalem for the Passover celebration paid a visit to Philip, who was from Bethsaida in Galilee. They said,

"Sir, we want to meet Jesus."

JOHN 12:20-21

COSMOS

Cosmos are agreeable, unfussy plants that grow in less-than-ideal soil. Their orange, pink, or white blooms resemble colorful daisies.

The Helper

The Holy Spirit helps us in our weakness. ROMANS 8:26

"CAN I HELP YOU?" How often has someone asked you that question when you truly needed assistance, but you simply replied, "That's fine—I can manage"? Or maybe later on a friend heard that you had needed help and inquired, "Why didn't you ask me?" But you brushed her aside, explaining, "I didn't want to trouble you." For many of us, talking like this is a way of life.

Unfortunately, we give similar answers to God as well. When the Holy Spirit offers us help, we say, by our actions if not by our words, "I can manage, thanks!" But as Christians, we shouldn't respond to God in such fashion—because Christians *know* they need the Holy Spirit's wisdom, guidance, comfort, and power to experience the abundant life Christ promised.

Paul learned this lesson the hard way. He had always been an independent guy, able to stand on his own feet. So God had to knock the independence out of him. Paul went through many hardships as a Christian (2 Corinthians 1:8; 11:21-29), but he recognized these things happened so he would stop relying on himself and learn "to rely only on God, who raises the dead" (2 Corinthians 1:9). Perhaps this is why we find so much emphasis in Paul's letters on the ways the Spirit helps us. He had learned he couldn't do life on his own.

*The Holy Spirit still wants to be our Helper, but there is a condition:
We must acknowledge our weakness! Only then can he come with his
strength, just as Jesus promised.*

"My grace is all you need. My power works best in weakness."
So now I am glad to boast about my weaknesses, so that the
power of Christ can work through me.

2 CORINTHIANS 12:9

PETUNIA

Technically perennials,
petunias are often planted as
annuals. Their trumpet-shaped
blossoms range from white
to purple and include
speckled and veined
varieties as well.

Always Beside You

Even when I walk through the darkest valley, I will not be afraid, for you are close beside me. PSALM 23:4

THERE ISN'T ONE OF US who likes going through hard times. Given the choice, we would certainly prefer a smooth and comfortable journey through life. Yet at some point, we will face illness, or pain, or bereavement, or marital challenges, or financial problems, or family strains . . . the list could go on. And even if we were to somehow escape these common struggles, we would certainly face death one day.

Yet in light of these challenges, God makes a promise—a promise to always *be there*, to always *be with us* in every situation, encouraging us in our difficulties, comforting us in sorrows, strengthening us when we are weak, helping us in times of need.

David went through some dreadful experiences on his journey to fulfill his calling to be king, but he found God's promised presence in them all and discovered the truth of our opening text—a verse that has helped millions over the centuries. Like David, Paul faced all sorts of hardships on his journey to fulfill his call to be an apostle; but he, too, found God's promised presence in them all, discovering for himself that "my grace is all you need. My power works best in weakness" (2 Corinthians 12:9).

Whatever situation you face, remember that God really is beside you. Take comfort in knowing that his presence will never fail to find you.

The LORD will personally go ahead of you. He will be with you;
he will neither fail you nor abandon you.

DEUTERONOMY 31:8

IMPATIENS BALSAMINA

Impatiens balsamina, or garden
balsam, was popular in Victorian
times. The Latin word *impatiens*
refers to the seed's impatient
push from its ripe pod.

Who Needs Church?

The church is his body; it is made full and complete by Christ,
who fills all things everywhere with himself. EPHESIANS 1:23

WHEN YOU ASK PEOPLE what they think of when they hear the word *church*, most replies will almost certainly involve a building associated with weddings or funerals or a weekly worship service.

But the Bible doesn't define *church* as either of those things! It describes the church as nothing less than a family: *God's* family, made up of all who put their faith in Jesus—a family that spreads through time and space; that cuts across boundaries of color, race, and class; and that bursts through even the barrier of death itself.

Of course, you don't have to be part of a church to be a Christian. Or do you? It seems the New Testament knows nothing of freelance Christians who drift here and there or nowhere. It knows nothing of Christians who claim to be part of "the" church without being part of "a" church.

And once we start to see what church really is, we can see why. For it's not only God's family but also a living expression of Christ's body, with all his life, love, and power flowing down from him as head to all the members. And that's why church is the sphere of exciting adventures with God and his people!

Don't neglect—and don't despise—the body of Christ. Resolve to be as committed to the church as he himself is. You need it—and it needs you.

All of you together are Christ's body,

and each of you is a part of it.

1 CORINTHIANS 12:27

SWEET WOODRUFF
Sweet woodruff is an herb
that makes a wonderful
ground cover and pairs well
with hostas and coral bells,
two other shade-
loving plants.

Rich in God

This same God who takes care of me will supply all your needs from his glorious riches, which have been given to us in Christ Jesus.

PHILIPPIANS 4:19

PROBABLY ALL OF US have moments when we think, *I wish I had a bit more money.* But how much more is enough? When does our desire for more stop? Yes, money is required to live, but focusing too much on money is a sure sign it's becoming our god.

Jesus said, "You cannot serve God and be enslaved to money" (Matthew 6:24), while Paul warned that "people who long to be rich fall into temptation and are trapped by many foolish and harmful desires that plunge them into ruin and destruction. For the love of money is the root of all kinds of evil" (1 Timothy 6:9-10). The Bible is not against money, of course. In fact, God often promises to provide for our needs, though not necessarily for our wants.

But the Bible also gives practical guidelines to help us keep money in perspective: It tells us to (1) get our money honestly, not through deceitful or shady practices; (2) use our money wisely by providing for ourselves and our family; (3) handle our money faithfully, understanding we're stewards, not owners, of what God has entrusted to us; and (4) share our money generously, remembering that "'God loves a person who gives cheerfully'" (2 Corinthians 9:7).

If you want to be rich—certainly in spirit and soul—then take some time to reflect on whether these four principles are firmly embedded in your own life today. When they are, God will provide!

Seek the Kingdom of God above all else, and live righteously, and he will give you everything you need.

MATTHEW 6:33

ASTILBE
An astilbe's fluffy plumes attract butterflies and helpful insects. Its flower spikes vary in height from twelve inches to three or four feet.

Brings Joy

The kind of sorrow God wants us to experience leads us away from sin and results in salvation. There's no regret for that kind of sorrow. But worldly sorrow, which lacks repentance, results in spiritual death. 2 CORINTHIANS 7:10

THE DEVIL IS ALWAYS QUICK to convince us that coming clean with God—what the Bible calls repentance—will be painful and embarrassing; that it will bring misery, not joy, and so it would be better to forget about it and quickly move on, as King David tried to do after committing adultery (2 Samuel 11).

And yes, repentance can feel painful at first—in fact, it's meant to! It's partly what helps us see that we were wrong and discourages us from repeating the behavior. But rather like a surgical procedure, while the wounding is brief, the healing is lasting—as King David himself discovered.

Of course, all this requires faith since the devil is bringing his lies and false promises. This is when we need to stand on truth, believing God really means it when he tells us in his Word that repentance is always the best—indeed the only—way to deal with sin, and that it always brings release and joy. His promise is that "'if you return to me, I will restore you so you can continue to serve me'" (Jeremiah 15:19).

Worldly sorrow—just moping over our sins—gets us nowhere. But genuine repentance brings God's forgiveness, peace, and joy. Is there something you have been avoiding repenting about? Don't delay any longer; deal with it today!

His anger lasts only a moment, but his favor lasts a lifetime!
Weeping may last through the night, but joy comes with the morning.

PSALM 30:5

ZINNIA

Easy-to-grow zinnias love
sun and heat and are quick
to bloom, eager to share
their bright, round
faces in a variety of
bold colors.

Our Faith

"You don't have enough faith," Jesus told them. "I tell you the truth, if you had faith even as small as a mustard seed, you could say to this mountain, 'Move from here to there,' and it would move. Nothing would be impossible." MATTHEW 17:20

AS YOU GET OLDER, once-firm muscles begin to weaken, and before you know it, you don't recognize the person staring back at you in the mirror. Something happens to our muscles along life's way! Our "faith muscles" aren't immune either. The longer we're Christians, the easier it is to stop "exercising" and become lazy.

Even the disciples discovered this to be true. Jesus had come down the mountain after the Transfiguration to learn they had experienced an embarrassing failure when they couldn't bring deliverance to a demonized boy. Jesus then healed the boy instantly. After they asked Jesus why they had floundered, he replied in the words of our opening passage.

Jesus had previously given the Twelve "authority to cast out evil spirits and to heal every kind of disease and illness" (Matthew 10:1), and they had gone out "preaching the Good News and healing the sick" (Luke 9:6).

But the disciples had forgotten that neither past authority nor past experiences are substitutes for present faith. Perhaps their very success had made them presumptuous, and in this situation they had neglected to have faith.

None of us ever gets to a stage where we can "settle down" and think that God will work in spite of our complacency. Avoid the trap the disciples fell into and exercise those faith muscles today!

It is impossible to please God without faith. Anyone who wants to come to him must believe that God exists and that he rewards those who sincerely seek him.

HEBREWS 11:6

COLUMBINE
Columbines are among a hummingbird's favorite flowers. These perennials are easy to grow but don't bloom until the second year when planted from seed.

SECURE
in His Hands

*My sheep listen to my voice; I know them, and they follow me.
I give them eternal life, and they will never perish. No one can
snatch them away from me, for my Father has given them to me, and
he is more powerful than anyone else. No one can snatch
them from the Father's hand.* JOHN 10:27-29

HAVE YOU EVER LOST AN ITEM THAT'S PRECIOUS TO YOU?
If so, you'll know how feelings of panic can arise as you desperately search for it, fearful your treasure may be gone forever.

Sometimes believers can become just as fearful of losing their relationship with God—often after they've committed a sin "once too often" or when they've fallen back into the same sinful habit that plagued them before they became a Christian.

At such times, the devil is quick to whisper in our ears, "That's it! You've lost your salvation. God will never forgive you now!" And all too often, we believe him. That's why it's so important to replace Satan's lies with Scripture's truths.

God makes a rock-solid promise to keep safe those who commit their lives to him. The reason he can do so is simple: It has nothing to do with us, but everything to do with Christ. His promises depend simply on his once-for-all sacrifice for us on the cross.

*Because of Jesus, we can be certain that we're secure in our Father's love.
So fear not: Nothing—and no one—can snatch you out of his hands!*

This is the will of God, that I should not lose even one of all those he has given me, but that I should

raise them up at the last day.

JOHN 6:35, 39

LILY OF THE VALLEY
Finland's national flower, lily of the valley, blossoms in spring. A member of the asparagus family, its sweetly scented blooms flourish in cool weather.

THE GOD
Who Guides

Trust in the LORD with all your heart; do not depend on your own understanding. Seek his will in all you do, and he will show you which path to take. PROVERBS 3:5-6

EVERY DAY, MILLIONS OF PEOPLE around the world abandon their usual scientific worldview and consult horoscopes, believing that somehow the positions of the planets can affect what happens to them.

When you think about it, it's crazy! It's not only crazy (as well as forbidden in Scripture) but also completely unnecessary because God himself—our heavenly Father—has promised to guide us. He doesn't just have plans; he has plans for *us*!

What an amazing thought that is! Jeremiah 29:11 says, "'I know the plans I have for you,' says the LORD. 'They are plans for good and not for disaster, to give you a future and a hope.'" And the God of all creation wants to guide us into those plans, as Proverbs 3:5-6 reminds us.

These plans aren't cold and deterministic. The Lord has already established the end goal, but still he invites us to partner with him in navigating the path toward that end goal (2 Corinthians 6:1). We can resist his will or respond to it; but if God doesn't get to us through the front door, he has a way of coming in through the back door!

God's promise today is that if we will set our hearts on him and ask for his help, he will guide and lead us further toward that goal he has planned for us. Trust him to lead you well along the journey.

I will guide you along the best pathway for your life.
I will advise you and watch over you.

PSALM 32:8

GOMPHRENA
Gomphrena blossoms are often used in Hawaiian leis because of their long-lasting blooms that retain color when dried. They're also great in cut-flower gardens.

COUNTING
the Cost

If any of you wants to be my follower, you must give up your own way,
take up your cross daily, and follow me. If you try to hang on to your life,
you will lose it. But if you give up your life for my sake,
you will save it. LUKE 9:23-24

ANYTHING WORTHWHILE IN LIFE has a cost. And if there isn't a cost—whether financial or in terms of commitment, time, or effort—then it's probably worth very little indeed. Following Jesus, too, has a cost.

This cost isn't that of atoning for our sins, however—Jesus paid that price in his once-for-all sacrifice on the cross, and there is absolutely nothing we can add to it.

No, this is the cost of following him, of learning how to live his way. It is the cost of being a disciple, with all the challenges to established loyalties that decision brings. Discipleship affects how we view our comforts, time, possessions, money, work, attitudes, values, goals—in short, everything!

That's why Jesus said we should first consider whether we're ready for all this. He said we need to be like someone who's planning a building project or a king who's going to war, asking, *Can I finish what I've started?* (Luke 14:28-33).

Jesus doesn't want us to make quick commitments, failing to take into account what we're getting ourselves into. Rather, he requires that we thoughtfully assess whether we're truly ready to follow him.

Today, count the cost—again! But be encouraged: Although the costs are real, the rewards are amazing!

Everyone who has given up houses or brothers or sisters or father or mother or children or property, for my sake, will receive a hundred times as much in return and will inherit eternal life.

MATTHEW 19:28-29

SCARLET SAGE

The scarlet sage, also called red salvia, adds a pop of color with its radiant red flowers. Deer and rabbits shun this plant's unique aroma.

HERE IS
Your God!

"Your God is coming!" Yes, the Sovereign LORD is coming in power. He will rule with a powerful arm. See, he brings his reward with him as he comes. ISAIAH 40:9-10

CHILDREN OFTEN ASK, "HOW BIG *IS* GOD?"—a question that has dumbfounded many parents! But actually, it's a question many of us ask, consciously or unconsciously, when problems come our way. Each of us wonders, *Is God big enough to deal with this? Does he have what it takes to meet my needs?*

The prophet Isaiah foresaw that God's people would ask the same questions when faced with God's judgment and exile for their sins. But he knew that if they could only see how big God is, they wouldn't ask such questions!

Isaiah 40 is a prophecy that despite their deserved punishment, God would come in great power to deal with his people's situation. Isaiah basically says, "Just look at creation and remember that those mighty oceans and mountains are as nothing to the LORD! Or look at the nations, seemingly so powerful, yet just a drop in a bucket to him.

"Or think of the stars—billions of them, all made by him and known to him. And you ask me if God is big enough to deal with *your* situation? Of course he is! He is God, who displays his majestic strength to help his children."

God has promised to be with you today and to come to your aid in every situation. With God on your side, nothing ever has the last word—not circumstances, nor fears, nor a grim medical prognosis; not even death itself. Whatever you may be facing, whatever opportunities or challenges lie ahead, the Sovereign God has your back, ruling in power.

The LORD your God is among you,

and he is a great and awesome God.

DEUTERONOMY 7:21

CANTERBURY BELL
Canterbury bells originated in southern Europe and can symbolize gratitude. Their Latin genus name, campanula, means "little bells."

THE FEAR OF
the LORD

Don't envy sinners, but always continue to fear the LORD.
You will be rewarded for this; your hope will not be disappointed.

PROVERBS 23:17-18

FEAR IS A POWERFUL EMOTION. At its best, it can save your life; at its worst, it leads to deception, destruction, and death. Yet there is a fear that always works for good and never for harm: It's what the Bible calls the "fear of the LORD."

Contrary to what you might be thinking, this phrase doesn't mean we should be afraid of God. Indeed, if we've trusted Jesus to forgive our sins and grant us eternal life, we don't need to fear; for "there is no condemnation for those who belong to Christ Jesus" (Romans 8:1).

Rather, to fear the LORD means to have proper respect for God. Yes, God wants us to be his friends, but we shouldn't reduce that relationship to the level of being buddies. Such a move would lead us to treat him lightly, and truly fearing the LORD is about living reverently in view of his glory and majesty.

As we do so, a number of blessings follow. Proverbs tells us that "fear of the LORD is the foundation of true knowledge" (1:7); "fear of the LORD lengthens one's life" (10:27); "fear of the LORD is a life-giving fountain" (14:27); "fear of the LORD teaches wisdom" (15:33); "true humility and fear of the LORD lead to riches, honor, and long life" (22:4); and that "by fearing the LORD, people avoid evil" (16:6).

It's little wonder we are urged to "always continue to fear the LORD"
(Proverbs 23:17). So be encouraged: You don't need to be afraid of God, but
take this opportunity to check on how healthy your respect for him is.

The LORD watches over those who fear him,

those who *rely on his unfailing love*.

PSALM 33:18

CROWN IMPERIAL
Crown imperials are well suited
to their name. These three-foot
stalks are "crowned" with eye-
catching clusters of blooms
and create beautiful focal
points in gardens.

TESTED
for a Purpose

*[God] knows where I am going. And when he tests me,
I will come out as pure as gold.* JOB 23:10

ASK MOST CHRISTIANS what the story of Job is about, and they'll answer, "Suffering." But while suffering is clearly an important aspect, the real issue isn't suffering, but righteousness.

One of Job's first questions was, "How can a person be declared innocent [or righteous] in God's sight?" (Job 9:2). He'd lived as righteously as he could—he was "just and blameless" (12:4)—and things still went badly for him.

Yet in the midst of his struggles, Job hung on in faith. Having lost his possessions and his children, Job's first response was, "I came naked from my mother's womb, and I will be naked when I leave. The LORD gave me what I had, and the LORD has taken it away. Praise the name of the LORD!" (1:21).

Later, when he was afflicted by painful sores, Job's wife encouraged him to curse God and die. He replied, "Should we accept only good things from the hand of God and never anything bad?" (2:10). And for the rest of the story, Job continues to trust God, despite all his struggles and questions.

Job's sufferings weren't an end in themselves. They were designed to drive him deeper into God; to help him see you could be the most righteous person on earth and still not deserve anything from God! Only when Job understands this does God restore him.

Maybe you are experiencing tough times at the moment. If so, remember this: It isn't because God has abandoned you; it is simply his testing—for your ultimate good. Keep trusting, and he will bring you through.

The Lord knows how to rescue godly people

from their trials.

2 PETER 2:9

PANSY

Pansies have been called the "flowers with faces." Their heart-shaped petals and cheery color combinations lend personality wherever they're planted.

Build My Church

*I say to you that you are Peter (which means "rock"), and upon this rock
I will build my church, and all the powers of hell will not
conquer it.* MATTHEW 16:17-18

LET'S FACE IT: Being part of a local church isn't always easy.
There are plenty of challenges, frustrations, and discouragements. But Matthew 16:18 assures us that no matter what, Jesus
will build his church—and *nothing* can stop him!

Such confidence isn't based on what may or may not have
happened in our own church situations, but on this certain
promise of Jesus. Your own church may be struggling to grow, or
perhaps it's even shrinking; meanwhile, the church in China, for
example, has grown by millions over the past several decades.

The church of Jesus *is* expanding! So don't be dismayed. He
has promised to build his church, and this is a promise he will
keep. Our part is not to worry about the growth; it is simply to
"seek the Kingdom of God above all else" (Matthew 6:33). If we will
make his Kingdom our first priority, Jesus will build his church.

And if you think about it, it's logical that Jesus will do so. After
all, the church was born out of nothing less than his death on the
cross. If it cost Jesus such a price to bring his church into being, do
we really think he will give up with the job only half done?

If you've felt discouraged recently with problems in your local church or shrinking attendance, take hold of Jesus' promise again. Above all, ask him how you can play your part in seeing his promise come to pass.

Feed and shepherd God's flock—his church, purchased with his own blood. ACTS 20:28

BERGENIA

Bergenias are sometimes called "pigsqueak" because of the sound their leaves make when rubbed together. Those large leaves work well in floral arrangements.

Cannot Forget

> *Can a mother forget her nursing child? Can she feel no love for the child she has borne? But even if that were possible, I would not forget you! See, I have written your name on the palms of my hands.*
>
> ISAIAH 49:15-16

THE WORLD IS FULL OF CYNICS—many of them professional, paid to write sneering columns in newspapers or to produce slanted views of life for TV or social media. But most cynics are just ordinary people who have become discouraged, or have lost their perspective, or have been disappointed once too often.

Sadly, even God's people can become cynical when things start to go wrong or if they believe God has forgotten about them. That's what was happening in the prophet Isaiah's day, and God addresses the issue in the Scripture above.

Think about it: Is God really so big, so great, so "out there" that he could forget us? Is he so busy running the world that it's impossible for him to remember our needs, which are small matters in the grand scheme of the universe? Of course not. Our God is simply too loving to behave in such a manner!

God cannot fail us because he cannot forget us. Unlike frail humanity, God never forgets, not even for a moment. He never switches off in the middle of our prayers or drifts into thinking about something else when we're talking to him.

If life has thrown you a curveball and you're tempted to become cynical, remember God's promise that your very name is engraved on the palms of his hands. You are safe and secure in his love!

I, the LORD, made you, and I will not forget you.

ISAIAH 44:21

ALLIUM

Allium blooms grow from bulbs and add an ornamental finishing touch to a garden bed, even after the tiny flowers dry up.

Stop and Think!

HAVE YOU EVER NOTICED that the little things in life can often be missed or taken for granted? They constantly perform their appointed tasks, but we often pay little attention until someone points them out.

Well, there's a little word in the Bible that is just like that: "Interlude"—or in Hebrew, *Selah*. It faithfully gets on with its work, but most of us ignore the significance of what it's calling us to do. You've probably skipped over reading it many times in the Psalms, as though it weren't important.

So what does "Interlude," or *Selah*, mean? The short answer is, We don't know! The word was probably a musical term or instruction to the choir, requiring a pause or change of key to emphasize what had just been sung. So a good translation might be, "Stop and think about that!" The psalmists didn't want God's people to simply pass on quickly to the next psalm; they wanted them to stop and think about the meaning behind the words they had just sung.

In our busy world, the admonition to "Stop and think!" is more relevant than ever. So rather than rush through your day, why not punctuate it with lots of Selah moments? Look at a tree, a cloud, a face, a child, a sunset, a star-filled sky, and say to yourself, Selah! Interlude! Just think about that! Enjoy each opportunity to give thanks to God.

Open up, ancient gates! Open up, ancient doors, and let the King of glory enter. Who is the King of glory? The LORD of Heaven's Armies—

he is the King of glory. Interlude

PSALM 24:9-10

CLEMATIS

Clematis are known as the "queen of climbers." Some varieties grow on long vines, but others thrive perfectly well in small gardens or pots.

WALKING AND
Watching

"What do you see, Amos?" he asked. I replied,
"A basket full of ripe fruit." Then the LORD said, "Like this fruit,
Israel is ripe for punishment!" AMOS 8:2

"LONG AGO GOD SPOKE many times and in many ways to our ancestors through the prophets" (Hebrews 1:1). God spoke to some of those prophets through visions, dreams, or an audible voice; but others heard God's message through what they saw—whether literally or in their minds' eye.

They were busy with daily life, walking here or there, when God suddenly interrupted their thoughts and asked, *What do you see?*—just like he did for Amos. Jeremiah was another prophet who heard God speaking to him in this way: "The LORD said to me, 'Look, Jeremiah! What do you see?'" (Jeremiah 1:11). As the prophets looked at what had caught their attention, they suddenly found God using common, everyday objects to communicate profound messages.

God still does the same today. The trouble is, we're often so busy that we just don't hear what he's saying, and we miss many opportunities to receive God's revelation or to hear what is on his heart.

But we can train ourselves to hear God better by simply *looking*. As we're going about our usual business, we can ask ourselves, *What do I see?* If we only stop and listen, we'll find God speaking again and again—not just in religious settings but also while out on a walk or standing by the sink or sitting in our offices.

For example, you suddenly see a rubber band, and for some

reason it grabs your attention. Before you know it, you hear God's voice speaking to your heart, saying, "Where does that rubber band end? Nowhere! So is my love for you!"

For some of the prophets, walking and watching were real keys to hearing God speak. Why can't it be the same for you?

Wake up and look around.

The fields are already ripe for harvest.

JOHN 4:34-35

ANEMONE
Delicate anemones
close at night and reopen
in the morning, symbolizing
relaxation and anticipation.
Red anemones symbolize
Jesus' blood shed for
our forgiveness.

the Promises

The LORD your God has increased your population, making you as numerous as the stars! And may the LORD, the God of your ancestors, multiply you a thousand times more and bless you as he promised! DEUTERONOMY 1:10-11

DEUTERONOMY WAS ONE OF Jesus' favorite books—we know because he quoted from it so often. Perhaps this was the case because Deuteronomy reminds us of God's faithfulness and our need to respond with our own faithfulness.

It begins with the Israelites standing on the edge of the Jordan River, and Moses reminding them how God had told them to leave Mount Sinai, where he had given them his law, and head for the land he had promised their ancestors long ago. The journey had taken them forty years; nevertheless, God's promise still stood.

What's interesting, however, is that as Moses gets further into his speech, he suddenly stops and blesses the people with the words of Deuteronomy 1:10-11, in which he asks God to fulfill his promise *even more* than he already had.

So often we fail to see God's power because, unlike Moses, we fail to pray his promises into being. We settle for simply hoping they will somehow work out. But God's promises aren't magic. They show us what is in his heart to do, but he wants us to claim those promises and work with him to see them come to pass. And prayer is such an important part of that.

Has God made promises to you in the past? Then pray them into being! Remember the story so far and be thankful—but then, like Moses, ask him for more!

I have been bold enough to pray this prayer to you because you have revealed all this to your servant.

2 SAMUEL 7:27

BALLOON FLOWER
Balloon flowers are native to China, Japan, Korea, and Siberia. Their purplish blooms expand before bursting open in bell-shaped flowers.

Falling Apart

It was in the year King Uzziah died that I saw the Lord.
He was sitting on a lofty throne, and the train of his robe
filled the Temple. ISAIAH 6:1

IT MUST HAVE SEEMED the world had fallen apart. After a glorious—and for those days, enormously long—reign of fifty-two years during which Judah had prospered, the godly king Uzziah had died. It's likely that all sorts of questions were running through people's minds: *Will the new king be as good? What will life be like for God's people? With King Uzziah no longer on the throne, what will happen to us now that Assyria, that superpower nation with territorial ambitions, is right on our doorstep?*

God's answer for Isaiah's anxiety was simple: It was a revelation of himself. The earthly king was gone, but *the* King, the King of glory, was still on *his* throne—high and exalted, holy and majestic, worshiped by the hosts of heaven; a king who was certainly not about to die! And it was seeing *this* king that reassured Isaiah, helped him make sense of everything, and caused him to take hold of God's promises for his people once again.

It's in encountering God ourselves—as the King seated on his throne, high above everything yet not so far removed that he can't deal with our sin and circumstances—that we, too, can stand firm in chaos. So don't be afraid to focus on the Lord's infinite power and majesty. When you do, truth comes into perspective, and you can take hold of his promises anew.

I saw a throne in heaven and someone sitting on it.

REVELATION 4:2

CELOSIA

Celosia plants are also known as cockscombs, brain celosia, and woolflowers. Different varieties can look like flames of fire or colorful brains.

THE GOD OF
All Comfort

All praise to God, the Father of our Lord Jesus Christ. God is our merciful Father and the source of all comfort. He comforts us in all our troubles so that we can comfort others. 2 CORINTHIANS 1:3-4

WHAT DO YOU THINK OF when you hear the word *comfort*? Settling down into your favorite armchair with a book? Escaping from the kids to soak in the bathtub for half an hour? Munching your way through a box of chocolates?

All these examples are common expressions of comfort. But the relief they provide quickly passes, and none come anywhere near what the Bible means by "comfort." For true comfort is nothing less than an invasion of God's encouragement and strength in demanding times—not just to bring temporary relief or to keep us going, but also to transform and energize us so we can emerge victorious—and then encourage others.

When his people were once feeling weary, God assured them, "I, yes I, am the one who comforts you" (Isaiah 51:12). And Jesus promised something even better: comfort from within. He said he would send "another Advocate [or Comforter], who will never leave you" (John 14:16)—the Holy Spirit—who lives within his children.

Of course, God knows we sometimes need encouragement "with skin on"—that is, in the form of a friend. So he will often send the right person to visit or contact us at just the right moment. He did this for Paul and Timothy, too: "God, who encourages those who are discouraged, encouraged us by the arrival of Titus" (2 Corinthians 7:6), leading Paul to write the opening Scripture above.

Whether directly or indirectly, God promises to be your comfort today, in every situation you face. Believe it, receive it—and then pass it on!

I will comfort you . . .

as a mother comforts her child.

ISAIAH 66:13

CHINESE HONEYSUCKLE

Known as Rangoon creeper, Chinese honeysuckle vines produce blooms that range from white to maroon. When grouped together, these colorful plants help reduce erosion.

AN ATTITUDE OF
Gratitude

Give thanks to the God of heaven.
His faithful love endures forever. PSALM 136:26

AFTER GIVING A PRESENT to someone, how would you feel if they told you, "What a lovely gift! Thank you so much!"—but then later you discovered they'd thrown it in the trash can? Not too happy! But that's exactly how God must feel when the "thanks" we express in worship aren't backed up by "thanks" expressed in our everyday lives.

God is looking for *an attitude of gratitude*: lives that exhibit constant gratefulness to God and to others; where our *first* response is gratitude rather than grumbling; where thankfulness permeates everything we are and do; where appreciation is the very atmosphere we breathe.

For most of us, this doesn't come instinctively. But we can work at it. For example, we can ensure that our prayer times are filled with gratitude and we aren't just asking for what's on our shopping lists. We can seek to be grateful in the daily run of life—at home, at work or school, in the store, on the bus—looking constantly to use those little words: *thank you*. And we can ensure that an attitude of gratitude pervades our conversations so people leave us feeling better rather than worse.

In short, we can discipline ourselves to become a people of thanks-living and not just thanks-giving.

Today, ask yourself, Do I model thanks-giving or thanks-living in my life? Do I seek to maintain an attitude of gratitude? Am I grateful or do I grumble? Today is as good a day as any to start approaching things differently!

Always be joyful. Never stop praying.

Be thankful in all circumstances, for this is God's will for you who belong to Christ Jesus. 1 THESSALONIANS 5:16-18

ALSTROEMERIA

Alstroemeria, named after Swedish botanist Klas von Alstroemer, symbolizes friendship and devotion. Its flowers are long lasting in a vase.

THE GOD OF
Holiness

[The seraphim] were calling out to each other, "Holy, holy, holy is the LORD of Heaven's Armies!" . . . Their voices shook the Temple. . . . Then I said, "It's all over! I am doomed, for I am a sinful man." ISAIAH 6:3-5

MANY OF US HAVE EXPERIENCED bathing and dressing up a baby in his best outfit, only to have Junior suddenly fill his diaper. And not just fill—but *fill*! You know, one of those "It's gone everywhere!" moments when everything within you cries, "Yuck! Such filth alongside such cuteness and cleanliness!"

And that's a pretty good picture of how God feels about sin. He is so clean, so pure, so holy that he can't even bear the sight or smell of it. And what he can't bear the sight of comes under his judgment.

Yet judgment isn't God's last word where sin is concerned! He doesn't simply tell us to be holy and leave us to get on with it; he himself makes us holy. That's what Isaiah discovered in his overwhelming vision of the holy God in his Temple. He wanted to run because he felt so dirty. But an angel touched his lips with a coal from the altar and said, "This coal has touched your lips. Now your guilt is removed, and your sins are forgiven" (Isaiah 6:7). God himself dealt with the problem!

We don't need to run from our holy God, even though our shortcomings may make us feel like doing so. No matter what we've said or done, or failed to say or do, God has promised to cleanse us through Christ's death, which provides full and final atonement for our sins. That forgiveness is still—and always—available.

*Don't run or hide or try to explain your sin away. Yes, it disgusts God;
but bring it to him and let him deal with it, just as he has promised.*

*I am the LORD
who makes you holy.*

LEVITICUS 20:8

HOLLYHOCK
Tall and cheerful-looking
hollyhocks are lovely in cottage-
style gardens. Painted lady
butterflies love these
midsummer bloomers.

with Jesus

[Jesus said,] "I no longer call you slaves. . . . Now you are my friends, since I have told you everything the Father told me." JOHN 15:15

WHAT A BLESSING IT IS to have a special friend—one with whom you can laugh and cry and really be yourself, whom you trust implicitly through thick and thin and who loves you enough to speak the truth.

Such is the kind of relationship that God wants with us. In fact, Jesus loved making friends—not so much with religious leaders (who actually found him difficult to be with) but with ordinary people. They felt utterly at ease in his presence, no matter what their past had been like. Helping others discover the friendship of God was one of Jesus' most important priorities.

Jesus' friendship was hardly ordinary, however. It was based on *covenant*. In Bible times, a covenant was a committed promise, an unbreakable contract that made someone "family." And God still desires to enter into a covenant with people today: one that can't—and won't—be broken, no matter what; one that draws us into his family and keeps us there.

Take heart, knowing that God wants you to experience this covenant with him in a fresh, new way. He invites you to be at ease in his presence and to share your day with him, whatever it may bring. He promises to be your friend. Enjoy!

We can rejoice in our wonderful new relationship
with God because our Lord Jesus Christ has made us

friends of God.

ROMANS 5:11

ACONITE

Poisoning can occur from
ingesting this wild plant;
yet aconite is often used as
a homeopathic medicine.
Its blossoms resemble the
hoods of medieval
monks.

the Weary

Even youths will become weak and tired, and young men will fall in exhaustion. But those who trust in the LORD will find new strength. They will soar high on wings like eagles. They will run and not grow weary. They will walk and not faint. ISAIAH 40:30-31

WEARINESS DOESN'T DISCRIMINATE. There are few who haven't experienced it—whether young mothers as they end the day or seniors as they start the day; whether manual laborers with aching limbs or executives with aching heads.

Each of us gets weary, when we've simply had enough and feel we just can't go on. And that's when it's good to remember that God himself never gets weary! Such a concept might be hard for us to grasp, but it's true. Even when God rested after Creation, it wasn't out of weariness; it was simply because his work was done.

God never gets weary. Isaiah wrote, "The LORD is the everlasting God, the Creator of all the earth. He never grows weak or weary" (Isaiah 40:28). And the psalmist said that "he who watches over Israel never slumbers or sleeps" (Psalm 121:4). But while this is all well and good for God, how do such truths affect *us*?

We may get weary—even if we are young and energetic—but as we trust in God each moment of the day, he shares his divine energy with us! Our weariness is exchanged for his strength, and we can soar above our pressures like eagles soaring above the earth. All we need to do is stop and call on that wonderful promise.

The God of Israel gives

power and strength to his people.

PSALM 68:35

DAHLIA
Dahlias offer an abundant return on a minimal investment. Numerous shades and sizes bloom in late summer and grow full and lush within one year.

THE DELIGHT OF
Discipline

Don't make light of the LORD's discipline, and don't give up when he corrects you. For the LORD disciplines those he loves, and he punishes each one he accepts as his child. HEBREWS 12:5-6

FEW OF US LIKE DISCIPLINE—at least when we're receiving it! Yet discipline plays an important part in shaping our lives. Any athlete knows that discipline is vital if they want to succeed; any parent knows they must discipline their children to avoid having spoiled brats. Discipline is good for us, and God thinks so too. He isn't afraid to discipline his children. Why? Because he's angry with us? No—because he loves us!

That's why the book of Hebrews—written to Christians experiencing discipline through opposition and persecution—talks about the blessings God's discipline conveys. It reminds them that "the LORD disciplines those he loves" (12:6); that discipline means he is accepting them "as his own children" (verse 7) and not as illegitimate children; that "God's discipline is always good for us" (verse 10); and that while it never seems pleasant at the time, discipline produces "a peaceful harvest of right living for those who are trained in this way" (verse 11).

If you've been going through hard times, God is simply treating you as his own child, with a promise of doing you good. Seek today to thank God for his care and cooperate with him in your circumstances. You won't regret it!

Consider the joy
of those corrected by God!

Do not despise the discipline of the Almighty when you sin.
For though he wounds, he also bandages. He strikes, but
his hands also heal.

JOB 5:17-18

RANUNCULUS
Picture-perfect ranunculi
resemble roses and bloom
in layers of delicate petals.
They're an elegant option for
weddings and high-end floral
arrangements.

I Am with You

One night the Lord spoke to Paul in a vision and told him,
"Don't be afraid! Speak out! Don't be silent! For I am with you, and no
one will attack and harm you, for many people in this city belong to me."

ACTS 18:9-10

ONE OF THE MOST LIFE-CHANGING promises we as Christians can confidently claim is that God is with us. And our confidence in this promise doesn't depend on how good or bad we've been—for the basis of God's presence is Christ's sacrifice on the cross. Nor does it depend on whether life is throwing obstacles at us, for our constant companion is also our shield and defender. He is with us—always!

Jesus knew how important grasping and keeping hold of such wonderful truths would be. As the disciples went out with the Good News, not everyone was ready to receive it. They were rejected, mocked, persecuted, and even killed because of their message about Jesus. That's why Jesus' very last promise to them, before returning to his heavenly Father, was "I am with you always, even to the end of the age" (Matthew 28:20).

Sure enough, Jesus was with the disciples through it all, and it was this certainty that kept them going. Paul, too, experienced many hardships and rejections; it's little wonder that at times he became downhearted. On one such occasion, Jesus spoke to him the words in Acts 18:9-10 above. Though simple, they gave Paul renewed strength and vision.

Look for the LORD to encourage and strengthen you. Whatever opportunities or challenges come along today, his promise still holds true: "I am with you!"

I am with you, and
I will take care of you.
I, the LORD, have spoken!

JEREMIAH 1:19

CLEOME

Cleomes are known as spider flowers because of their clusters of radiating petals and fernlike foliage. Hummingbirds love them, and deer avoid them.

Stand Firm!

Put on every piece of God's armor so you will be able to resist the enemy in the time of evil. Then after the battle you will still be standing firm. EPHESIANS 6:13

CHRISTIANS OFTEN FALL into one of two camps when it comes to thinking about the devil and demons. Some, unable to accept anything that science cannot explain, dismiss the existence of demons as merely a primitive worldview, while others find demons under every bed and behind every problem. But somewhere between these extremes, real warfare is happening—a warfare which we need to be aware of but not afraid of.

When Jesus came to earth, he entered a battle zone, for the devil had no intention of giving up conquered territory. From his birth to his death, Jesus was opposed by Satan at every turn—sometimes through literal demons, but more often through the people and political and religious institutions that Satan controlled (Ephesians 6:12).

Yet the battle wasn't just his—it's ours, too! In fact, Jesus warned his followers they would be opposed: "I am sending you out as sheep among wolves. . . . You will stand trial before governors and kings because you are my followers" (Matthew 10:16, 18). And the fight will continue until Jesus returns, which is why Paul tells us in Ephesians 6:13 to put on our spiritual armor.

*The good news is this: **We know who wins!** For at the cross, Christ "disarmed the spiritual rulers and authorities"* (Colossians 2:15). *So today, don't focus on the devil; focus on Jesus! As you do, you will be able to stand firm.*

Stay alert! Watch out for your great enemy, the devil. He prowls around like a roaring lion, looking for someone to devour.

Stand firm against him,

and be strong in your faith.

1 PETER 5:8-9

HYDRANGEA

When mornings are sunny and shade cools the afternoons, hydrangea shrubs can grow large, displaying stunning globes of blooms in eye-catching colors.

Forgiven People

Oh, what a miserable person I am! Who will free me from this life that is dominated by sin and death? Thank God! The answer is in Jesus Christ our Lord. ROMANS 7:24-25

THERE YOU ARE, a born-again Christian, living your life for Jesus, when suddenly you say, think, or do something sinful. You're shocked! *Have I been playacting, not really living as a Christian all along?* you wonder. *Have I been deceiving myself? Have I become the hypocrite I've accused others of being?*

Fortunately, the answer is no. You have simply discovered the reality of living as a forgiven person in a fallen world. And you're not on your own: The truth is, all of God's people—even the most "sanctified"—fall at times. In fact, some of the greatest characters in the Bible failed God terribly at points in their lives—even so much that if they hadn't, we would have a very thin Bible indeed! Stories abound of them deceiving, lying, scheming, cheating, doubting, denying—even murdering. And yet God still used them.

Paul certainly experienced an inner struggle against sin at times, as he outlines in Romans 7. He didn't always act the way he wanted to. But he also knew the answer to this struggle: keeping his eyes on Jesus, who alone could rescue him.

Don't let the devil convince you that your sin has written you off! Like Paul, come to Jesus and find fresh forgiveness and commissioning for each new day.

David confessed to Nathan, "I have sinned against the LORD." Nathan replied, "Yes, but the LORD has forgiven you, and you won't die for this sin."

2 SAMUEL 12:13

CYCLAMEN
Cyclamen, whose flowers resemble hovering butterflies, are cool-season plants native to the eastern Mediterranean. They bloom around Thanksgiving and Christmas and go dormant during summer.

THE VALUE OF
Friendship

*Two people are better off than one, for they can help each other
succeed. If one person falls, the other can reach out and help.
But someone who falls alone is in real trouble.* ECCLESIASTES 4:9-10

THE BIBLE CONTAINS such lofty themes. But occasionally it
surprises us by coming down to earth with thoughts that seem
so . . . ordinary! Paul, for example, explored incredible mysteries
in his letters; yet in 2 Corinthians he wrote, "I had no peace of
mind because my dear brother Titus hadn't yet arrived" (2:13) and
"God, who encourages those who are discouraged, encouraged
us by the arrival of Titus" (7:6).

How perfectly human to worry about a friend who was missing and to cheer up when he arrived! Paul clearly understood the
value of friendship. True friends not only encourage and stand by
us but also aren't afraid to tell us the truth. And if we are wise, we
will listen. Proverbs 27:6 says, "Wounds from a sincere friend are
better than many kisses from an enemy."

The Bible demonstrates God's heart for friendship by portray-
ing several examples: Ruth and Naomi; David and Jonathan;
Jesus, Mary, and Martha; Paul and Timothy. And with so many
commands to love one another, the New Testament paints a clear
picture of the church as first and foremost a place of friendship.

Today, thank God for your friends. Pray for them and express your appreciation in tangible ways. And don't sit waiting for others to come and befriend you; instead, go and find someone whom you can be a friend to. In these ways, you can boldly play your part in making the church a place of friendship.

A friend is always loyal,
and a brother is born to help in time of need.

PROVERBS 17:17

AUBRIETA
Purple or blue aubrietas grow abundantly as ground cover for rock gardens and pathways. They're also ideal for gracing stone walls.

Strength

*The Sovereign LORD is my strength! He makes me as surefooted
as a deer, able to tread upon the heights.* HABAKKUK 3:19

"LORD, GIVE ME STRENGTH!" How often have you said or
heard that phrase? Usually it's just a cry of exasperation rather
than a genuine prayer. Yet it's a prayer that God is more than
happy to hear. The Bible is full of promises of strength for those
who come to God acknowledging they have no strength of
their own.

The prophet Habakkuk is a good example. Despite his many
questions amid the tough times Judah was facing, he declared he
could find strength in God. Habakkuk compared it to the kind of
strength that led a deer to dart swiftly across Judah's rocky hills,
never for one moment doubting it would slip.

Paul found this same strength in many situations. His apos-
tolic ministry brought incredible challenges—mental, physical,
and spiritual—but he came through them by simply focusing
on God and looking to him for strength. Even in the face of an
uncertain future while under house arrest, Paul confidently wrote
to the Philippian church, "I can do everything through Christ,
who gives me strength" (Philippians 4:13).

Perhaps today you're weary and at the end of your own resources as you face insoluble problems, fierce opposition, or overwhelming challenges. You may feel incapable of carrying on and ready to give up. Whatever your situation, remember that God promises to be your strength. You just need to turn to him and ask. He is faithful!

God has come to save me.

I will trust in him and not be afraid. The LORD GOD is my strength and my song; he has given me victory.

ISAIAH 12:2

SCABIOSA

The scabiosa, or pincushion flower, was named after the Latin word *scabious* because of the belief that its rough leaves could heal the scabies rash.

Forgiving

> *When you are praying, first forgive anyone you are holding*
> *a grudge against, so that your Father in heaven*
> *will forgive your sins, too.*
>
> MARK 11:25

HOW MUCH DO WE appreciate God's forgiveness? Sometimes it's hard to find the right words to answer that question. But not only is it hard to put our appreciation into words, it can be even harder to put it into practice. That's why Jesus said that one tangible measure of how much we really appreciate God's forgiveness is how forgiving we are of others.

Jesus said there is no place in the lives of his followers for anger or judgmental attitudes toward people who are simply as flawed as we are; no place for harboring feelings of resentment against those who have wronged us; no place for clinging to old wounds and grievances. For if we have truly understood God's forgiveness, then we the forgiven will also forgive.

But finding the grace to actually implement this can often be hard, right? When we're listening to a sermon about forgiveness, it's easy to believe we'll follow through on Jesus' teaching; yet in real life, forgiving is much more challenging. But it's there that we see how God's promises really work!

If you've been struggling with forgiveness, realize that God's grace for this challenge can be found today. Ask him to help you let go of all hurt and offense, and then make the decision (for that's what it comes down to) to forgive. As you do, Jesus said, you will truly know what it is to be forgiven.

If you forgive those who sin against you, your heavenly Father will forgive you. But if you refuse to forgive others, your Father will not forgive your sins.

MATTHEW 6:14-15

CARNATION

Carnation colors reflect unique meanings: light red for admiration, dark red for love, pink for gratitude or motherly love, purple for capriciousness, and yellow for rejection or disappointment.

AN UNSHAKABLE
Kingdom

> *Since we are receiving a Kingdom that is unshakable,*
> *let us be thankful and please God by worshiping*
> *him with holy fear and awe.*
>
> HEBREWS 12:28

ASK ANY MOM CHEERING her child's team along if she would mind it if they lost, and you will undoubtedly get this answer: "We all love to be winners!" There's far more satisfaction in saying "Great news—our team won!" than "Bummer—our team lost." And that's exactly how it is for us as Christians; as members of a team that is unstoppable, unbeatable, and absolutely assured of winning, we desire success!

The team we belong to is the Kingdom of God. This is a Kingdom, Jesus told us in Matthew 13, whose growth can't be stopped and whose reach is all-embracing. There is nothing that can overcome it, and there is no aspect of life it can't touch and transform. Like a mighty multinational corporation, God's Kingdom has a pervading influence that impacts people "from every tribe and language and people and nation" (Revelation 5:9). This is a Kingdom on the march, destined to be utterly victorious! Human kingdoms may rise and fall, but God's will never fail.

Be confident today that no matter what situations you might face, you are part of an unshakable Kingdom. You are on the winning side!

The world has now become the Kingdom
of our Lord and of his Christ, and

he will reign forever and ever.

REVELATION 11:15

CROCUS

Crocuses are among the first
bulbs to bloom and welcome
spring. As long as they have
sunshine, they're okay
with cool weather.

God Alone

I am the LORD your God, who rescued you from the land of Egypt, the place of your slavery. You must not have any other god but me.

EXODUS 20:2-3

EXODUS 20:2-3 COMES at the beginning of the Ten Commandments, which God gave to the Israelites shortly after they had been freed from slavery in Egypt, a land full of false gods and idols. It's a command to shun every false god and worship the one true God. What had framed their past was not to frame their future; the LORD alone was now to be their God. And this commandment would be repeated again and again in Israel's history, especially when the Israelites were enticed by the Canaanites' highly sensuous worship of gods and idols they believed would bring fertility to their land.

For us these days, worshiping a stone or wooden carving isn't an issue; but less obvious forms of idolatry certainly are. Whatever we give most of our energy, passion, and time to is our idol; for as Jesus put it, "Wherever your treasure is, there the desires of your heart will also be" (Luke 12:34). Common idols today include things like our homes, our families, our vacations, our hobbies, and our favorite football teams and social media apps. None of these are bad—but each is bad if it has the number one place in our lives. For whenever we put any of them first, through our time or affections, we have just worshiped an idol. And we are commanded to worship God alone.

If the Holy Spirit is nudging you about something that has gradually pushed God from the number one place in your life, then repent quickly and put God alone back at the center!

Worship only God!

REVELATION 22:9

BELLFLOWER
Bellflowers are cups of brightness with their upturned bell shapes and cheery blooms in purple, blue, white, and pink. They're hardy in cooler climates.

THE GOD WHO
Gives Hope

Lord, where do I put my hope? My only hope is in you. PSALM 39:7

HOW MANY TIMES have you heard someone say, "I'm keeping my fingers crossed" or "I hope things turn out okay"? But how on earth can putting one finger over another, or just hoping, make the least bit of difference in affecting what happens in life? Where *real* hope is found is in the living God!

That's what David, who wrote Psalm 39, discovered. He went through many hardships in life—situations that, from a human point of view, seemed quite hopeless. For example, though he was liked by King Saul at first, David soon found himself on the run once Saul saw him as a potential rival. David then had to spend some ten years fleeing from Saul, hiding in deserts, hills, and caves. At one point he even took refuge among Israel's enemies the Philistines, pretending to be insane in order to save his life. And even after David finally became king after Saul's death, life didn't always go smoothly for him. On one occasion he faced a civil war that drained him of all hope and caused him to flee.

But despite all the difficulties and challenges, David never gave up hope, for he knew the God of hope. "My only hope is in you," he would say again and again; and every time, he found that God was true to his promise as he rescued David from whatever opposed him.

Today, this same God of hope is with you—whatever you are facing.

Why am I discouraged? Why is my heart so sad?

I will put my hope in God!

I will praise him again—

my Savior and my God!

PSALM 42:5-6

HONEYSUCKLE

Honeysuckle vines are famous
for their signature fragrance
and tasty nectar. You'll find
them climbing up trellises and
fences or preventing erosion
as ground cover.

Priceless!

God paid a ransom to save you from the empty life you inherited from your ancestors. And it was not paid with mere gold or silver, which lose their value. It was the precious blood of Christ, the sinless, spotless Lamb of God. 1 PETER 1:18-19

HARDLY A MONTH PASSES without reports of a fantastic sum being paid for a priceless work of art. Often people pay millions of dollars. But for what? At one level, just a few strokes of paint on canvas or a chunk of marble sculpted into some form. So why are people willing to pay outlandish prices for such things? Because, quite simply, it's worth it to them.

And that really sums up why God paid such an amazing price for our redemption—because he felt we were worth it! He loved us so much that—even "while we were still sinners"—he was prepared to pay the ultimate price: the death of his own dear Son. He couldn't forgive us by simply saying, "Let's just forget about it." Sin has a price . . . an incredible price. And God sent his Son to pay it for us because he knew the cost was way outside anyone's budget!

God's incredible love for you led him to pay your sin penalty with the costliest possession he had—his priceless Son! Be encouraged that this is how much he is committed to you. And remember: If God gave Jesus in exchange for you, he will certainly provide everything else you need to live for him.

God showed his great love for us

by sending Christ to die for us while we were still sinners.

ROMANS 5:8

BEE BALM

Bee balm is native to North America and thrives in woodlands. Bees, butterflies, and hummingbirds love it. Picking these flowers encourages more to grow.

What a Savior!

The LORD your God is living among you.
He is a mighty savior. ZEPHANIAH 3:17

NOWADAYS, A "SAVIOR" is someone who rescues a troubled business or failing soccer team, or a friend who turns up and saves you from a crisis. But a savior in the religious sense . . . well, that's just old-fashioned and hardly relevant to life today, right? But if we find ourselves thinking that way, we've been robbed! The words *savior* and *salvation* need to be put back where they belong: in the realm of our daily walk with God.

In the Bible, salvation is never purely a spiritual concept; it is also a practical one. Nor is it an intangible concept; it is always specific. So we find people being saved *from* something and *into* something. It includes, among other things, salvation from sin, lack, despair, sickness, defeat, and Satan's kingdom of darkness—and into the very opposite: forgiveness, provision, hope, health, victory, and Jesus' Kingdom of light. This is far broader than just being saved from sin, period—which is what many Christians limit it to.

So how about you? Do you really believe God can save you from *everything*? Do you anticipate his salvation in your family, health, circumstances, plans, and work, or is your faith for salvation restricted to sin alone? And do you look to your own resources and abilities in daily life before looking to God, relegating him to little more than a last resort? Or is he the first one you turn to in every situation?

Today, don't try to be your own savior—that's God's job, and his delight!

I, yes I, am the LORD, and there is

no other Savior.

ISAIAH 43:11

SNAPDRAGON
Snapdragons are lush, medium-height flowers that can balance taller and shorter plants in a garden. Their ruffled blooms add beauty outdoors or in a vase.

through Failure

*Simon, Simon, Satan has asked to sift each of you like wheat.
But I have pleaded in prayer for you, Simon,
that your faith should not fail.*

LUKE 22:31-32

THERE ARE FEW WORTHWHILE TASKS in life that we can do (or at least do well) on our first try. When we were young, even mastering basics like eating, speaking, and writing required several attempts. As to more complex matters—well, for some of us, those took forever!

Life as a Christian is no different. The Bible describes becoming a Christian as being "born again" (John 3:3), and just like babies, we need to learn lots of skills to help us in our new lives. But those skills don't always come easily. This process of challenge and change is called discipleship, and it's a process that never ends. For discipleship isn't a course; it's a lifestyle.

By its very nature, discipleship involves failure—and that's something most of us find hard! Our society is geared toward success, and failures are dealt with mercilessly. Yet Jesus' disciples often failed! They failed to understand him, trust him, obey him, believe him, love him. But such is the very heart of discipleship: learning through failure. The issue is not "Have we failed?" but "Have we learned?"

No matter how many times his disciples failed him, Jesus never gave up on them. He lovingly and patiently kept working with them until they got it right. And that is his commitment to you today.

Then, as I looked and thought about it, I learned this lesson . . .

PROVERBS 24:32

BLEEDING HEART
Stems of the bleeding heart plant appear heavy and dripping, with rows of heart-shaped flowers in rich shades of pink, red, and white.

TEAR UP
the List!

Love . . . keeps no record of being wronged. 1 CORINTHIANS 13:4-5

HAVE YOU NOTICED how easy it is to keep mental lists of the wrongs people have done to you? Even when we try to forget, our wonderful inbuilt computers (our brains) have a way of remembering. But the Bible urges us to tear up all those lists!

Of course, everything within us usually feels we have a right to keep them, especially when we've been hurt. Peter thought he was being incredibly spiritual when he told Jesus he was prepared to shorten his mental list in the future to just seven offenses (in Judaism, the number seven symbolizes perfection). But Jesus' answer shocked him. He told Peter to forgive "not seven times . . . but seventy times seven!" (Matthew 18:22)—that is, endlessly!

Or to put it another way, he was telling Peter, "Just don't even keep lists! Forgiveness isn't something we can count up; it's the very atmosphere of God's Kingdom. True forgiveness means tearing up the list and leaving matters in God's capable hands."

What about you? Do you have any mental lists that detail how others have hurt, disappointed, or wronged you? If so, tear them up today. Let God deal with the issues and the people. He'll do a far better job than you could anyway!

Never pay back evil with more evil. Do things in such a way that everyone can see you are honorable.

Do all that you can to live in peace with everyone.

Dear friends, never take revenge. Leave that to the righteous anger of God. For the Scriptures say, "I will take revenge; I will pay them back," says the LORD.

ROMANS 12:17-19

ANGELONIA GOYAZENSIS
Angelonia goyazensis has snapdragon-like blooms and grows to approximately eighteen inches tall. Some think its foliage smells like apples.

Seems Distant

My God, my God, why have you abandoned me?
Why are you so far away when I groan for help? PSALM 22:1

WHEN LIFE IS TOUGH, it's easy to think, *Where is God in all this?* Even the psalmists had times when it seemed God was a million miles away, and they didn't hesitate to tell him so, as Psalm 22 shows.

But while such times can feel lonely—even scary—they can actually be precious. They can strengthen our faith, for we must learn to trust even when we cannot "feel." Difficult experiences remind us not to take God for granted, to remember that he is the Lord of glory, not just some friend who comes around when needed; and they allow hidden matters of the heart to come to the surface, where God can deal with them. But remember: Even if we don't feel God's presence, there is nowhere that his presence cannot be found; so we needn't fear he has left us.

Jesus quoted the opening words of Psalm 22:1 when he was suffering on the cross and experiencing the weight of the world's sin (Matthew 27:46). He felt completely abandoned by his Father. But he knew that he wasn't, for other cries followed: "It is finished!" (John 19:30) and "Father, I entrust my spirit into your hands!" (Luke 23:46)—cries of victory and trust. Jesus' death and his resurrection three days later assure us that as we trust in our heavenly Father, we will never be cut off from him.

No matter how you might feel today, God really is right there with you. The Cross is your assurance!

I can never escape from your Spirit!

I can never get away from your presence!

PSALM 139:7

DAME'S ROCKET
Like its relative arugula, the leaves of dame's rocket plants are edible. Their four-petal, usually violet flowers often are mistaken for phlox, which have five petals.

All Glory to God!

All glory to God, who is able to keep you from falling away and will bring you with great joy into his glorious presence without a single fault. All glory to him who alone is God, our Savior through Jesus Christ our Lord. All glory, majesty, power, and authority are his before all time, and in the present, and beyond all time! Amen. JUDE 1:24-25

OUR OPENING SCRIPTURE is an example of a *doxology*. The term comes from two Greek words: *doxa* ("glory") and *logos* ("word" or "speech"). So a doxology is an exclamation of praise glorifying God, and we find lots of them in the Bible. While such prayers are often used liturgically in church services today, we find them in the Bible in a variety of circumstances—from birth (Luke 1:68-79) to death (see Job 1:21)—and even in the ordinary routines of everyday life.

One example is when the sad story of Naomi and Ruth comes to its happy conclusion as Ruth marries Boaz and gives birth to a son (who will one day become the grandfather of King David). The women of the town spontaneously exclaim, "Praise the LORD, who has now provided a redeemer for your family!" (Ruth 4:14). Doxologies like the one above from Jude 1:24-25 are found frequently in the New Testament letters of Paul (e.g., 1 Timothy 1:17) and Peter (e.g., 2 Peter 3:18). Look for them when reading your Bible!

God's people were never afraid to let their spontaneous praise to him be known, whatever the circumstances and whoever was around. What about you?

Now all glory to God our Father forever and ever! Amen.

PHILIPPIANS 4:20

BROWALLIA

Amethyst flower and sapphire flower are two nicknames for browallia, whose bright purple and blue star-shaped blooms contrast beautifully with its vibrant green leaves.

CALLED TO

Be Disciples

Come, follow me, and I will show you how to fish for people! MARK 1:17

JESUS ISN'T INTERESTED in people becoming Christians. Are you shocked by that? Well, it's true. Jesus doesn't want *Christians*—he wants *disciples*. And this call to discipleship lay at the very heart of his ministry. It's how it began as he called those fishermen by the shores of the lake, and it's how it ended as he sent out those same men three years later to "go and make disciples of all the nations" (Matthew 28:19).

In the intervening years, Jesus had called all sorts of people to be disciples: fishermen, tax collectors, homemakers, freedom fighters, prostitutes—a whole cross section of society. There really was room for everyone in Jesus' school of discipleship. And in following him, their lives were changed.

Discipleship is still what Jesus wants today. It's a call to three things: First, to *decision*. When Jesus said, "Come!" a decision had to be made that would change the life of the one who made it. Second, a call to *difference*, for we can't follow while staying where we are or how we are. Third, a call to *destiny*, for discipleship is Jesus' tool for bringing us into God's eternal purposes for our lives.

For all who will pick up the challenge, the call and its promise are as real, as powerful, as effective as they were two thousand years ago. So how are you responding to Jesus' call, "Come, follow me"?

As Jesus left the town, he saw a tax collector named Levi sitting at his tax collector's booth.

"Follow me and be my disciple,"

Jesus said to him. So Levi got up, left everything, and followed him.

LUKE 5:27-28

MORNING GLORY

Related to sweet potatoes, quick-growing morning glories are drought-tolerant vines with heart-shaped leaves and trumpet-shaped blooms. These low-maintenance beauties attract hummingbirds and butterflies.

Our Generous God

He has showered his kindness on us, along with all
wisdom and understanding. EPHESIANS 1:8

WE ALL LOVE GENEROSITY—as long as we're on the receiving end! In Matthew 20:1-16, Jesus tells a parable that touches on this attitude: A kind landowner went out one morning to look for laborers and agreed to pay them a fair wage—a day's pay for a day's work. As the day went on, he became more and more generous. He kept going out to find yet more laborers; and each of them, regardless of how long he had worked, was paid a full day's wages too. The landowner gave them what they needed to support their families, not what they deserved on a strict hourly rate.

Those who didn't start work till five o'clock were really excited by such generosity, but those who had started at nine o'clock complained it wasn't fair. Yet the landowner wasn't being unfair; he was simply being incredibly generous. And his generosity had exposed the hearts of mean-minded people.

Through this story, Jesus was showing his disciples what God is like—incredibly generous. Today, the riches of his grace in Christ are freely promised and freely available to all, regardless of who we are or what we have done, regardless of whether we deserve them or not. And in fact, none of us do.

The miracle of grace is that our generous God doesn't deal with us according to what we deserve or feel we have earned, but simply according to his kindness. So call upon his generosity today!

If you sinful people know how to give good gifts to your children, how much more will your heavenly Father give good gifts to those who ask him.

MATTHEW 7:11

PERIWINKLE

Periwinkle, with its small star-shaped bluish flowers, is excellent for ground cover and erosion control. It also has been a go-to herbal remedy for centuries.

Your Destiny

> *God decided in advance to adopt us into his own family by bringing us to himself through Jesus Christ. This is what he wanted to do, and it gave him great pleasure.* EPHESIANS 1:5

WHEN WE HEAR the word *destiny*, we tend to think of great men and women who have changed the course of history or impacted countless lives. But the Bible says that all of us—ordinary people!—have a destiny too.

God's destiny for us, according to Ephesians 1:5, is to be adopted into his family, "the family of faith" (Galatians 6:10). As such, "together with Christ we are heirs of God's glory" (Romans 8:17). But while that is our general destiny, each of us has a particular destiny as well. And finding that destiny is about finding what we were made for.

Yet here's what surprises many Christians: That destiny doesn't have to be "spiritual"! In the film *Chariots of Fire*, based on the life of 1924 Olympic Gold Medalist Eric Liddell, Eric says he feels God's pleasure when he runs. In doing what he is made for, his true self is being realized.

For Eric, it was running; but for others it might be writing, painting, managing, serving, homemaking, or raising kids. Yes, ordinary things like these—and not just serving in Sunday school—can be our destinies in God.

If you've not yet discovered what your own destiny is, start seeking God about it. It will often be linked with those activities you enjoy doing most and are most fulfilled and fruitful in. Ask God to make you even more fruitful in these areas, and so enter more and more into the destiny that God has for you.

I press on to possess that perfection

for which Christ Jesus first possessed me.

PHILIPPIANS 3:12

AGERATUM
The hardy blooms of the ageratum, or floss flower, can be pink, purple, white, or blue, which works well in patriotic arrangements.

Beautiful Feet!

Everyone who calls on the name of the LORD will be saved.

ROMANS 10:13

WE ONLY HAVE TO WATCH the news to see what a mess the world is in. At every level—politically, economically, morally, and spiritually—the human race seems to lurch from bad to worse. Of course, the world's basic problem is not economics or politics or ecology, but sin—which leads to all the other stuff. Yet despite this dark picture, the promise of Romans 10:13 still proves true. That's where beautiful feet come in!

For people to be saved, they first need to hear the Good News about Jesus that can save them, which means we must go and tell it to them. Paul writes, "How can they hear about him unless someone tells them? And how will anyone go and tell them without being sent? That is why the Scriptures say, 'How beautiful are the feet of messengers who bring good news!'" (Romans 10:14-15).

God is still looking for those who will believe his message about beautiful feet! This doesn't mean we have to go to some far-flung nation; the mission begins right on our own doorstep—among our own unsaved family, neighbors, friends, and colleagues.

Why not claim God's promise of having "beautiful feet"? That is, of people thinking it was fantastic that you shared the Good News of Jesus with them, which alone can rescue them from our messed-up world. God's heart is to see everyone saved. Are you playing your part by being one of his messengers?

We work hard and continue to struggle,

for our hope is in the living God,

who is the Savior of all people and particularly of all believers.

1 TIMOTHY 4:10

GARDENIA

Humidity-loving gardenias symbolize appealing characteristics such as sweetness, purity, and joy. Their creamy-white flowers and glossy green foliage give them an elegant appearance.

Slowing Down

May the words of my mouth and the meditation of my heart be pleasing to you, O LORD, my rock and my redeemer. PSALM 19:14

LIFE IS SO BUSY that few of us take time to slow down, stop, and think. We know we need to; but the day's demands just seem to press in and crowd out the space to pause. Yet stopping and thinking is exactly what the Bible encourages us to do. Psalm 19:14 calls this "meditation." *Meditation* is about reflecting in depth and at length, focusing on one thing and shutting the door to everything else that fights to crowd into our thoughts—even good things.

That's what Mary did when Jesus visited her home. Martha, Mary's sister, busied herself preparing dinner—a good and reasonable task, but not the best one. Jesus told her, "There is only one thing worth being concerned about. Mary has discovered it, and it will not be taken away from her" (Luke 10:42).

Stopping isn't always easy, though. Our minds so quickly get distracted. The Psalms suggest at least three things we can meditate on: God's law (Psalm 1:2), God's love (Psalm 48:9), and God's works (Psalm 77:12). You could start out by choosing just one Bible verse or aspect of God's character or creation to help you stop, focus, and be drawn deeper into him.

Biblical meditation isn't a relaxation technique; it's an expression of relationship with, and dependence on, God. Yes, your life is busy today, just like Martha's was. But why not take a few minutes right now to stop and think about him? He really is wonderful; just meditate on that!

O God, we meditate on your unfailing love as we worship in your Temple. PSALM 48:9

RED VALERIAN
Kiss-me-quick, fox's brush, devil's beard, and Jupiter's beard are other names for the red valerian. Leaves and roots are tasty in salads.

LITTLE FAITH,
Big God!

If you had faith even as small as a mustard seed, you could say to this mulberry tree, "May you be uprooted and be planted in the sea," and it would obey you! LUKE 17:6

WE CAN SOMETIMES THINK of God's promises as so huge that they must be too good to be true—especially for ordinary people like us. During those times, we need to remember that God's promises don't depend on us; they depend on him! What matters isn't the smallness of our faith but the bigness of our God.

If we think it's the size of our faith that makes things happen, we'll give up before we start, or get weary halfway through, or believe the devil's accusations and drop the whole idea. But when the disciples felt challenged by their own lack of faith, Jesus said that all they needed was faith the size of a tiny mustard seed.

The issue isn't the amount of faith, but the object of faith; not how much faith we've got, but where the faith that we do have is focused. To put it another way, there is no power in "faith"; there is only power in Jesus. Faith needs to be faith in him, not faith in "faith." It's not faith that brings about the fulfillment of God's promises; it's Jesus! Faith is simply what keeps us focused on him. And that's why we can hold on to God's promises, for it's ultimately about him, not us.

Whatever promise you are waiting for, let your faith today be focused on your God, not on your faith!

All who put their faith in Christ share the same blessing Abraham received because of his faith. GALATIANS 3:9

PEONY

Peonies are perennials that outlast a lifetime, even surpassing a hundred years. Enormous blooms, delightful fragrance, and an undemanding nature make them a favorite.

Then We Are Strong

> *You come to me with sword, spear, and javelin, but I come to you in the name of the LORD of Heaven's Armies—the God of the armies of Israel, whom you have defied. Today the LORD will conquer you. . . . And the whole world will know that there is a God in Israel!*

1 SAMUEL 17:45-46

TODAY'S OPENING SCRIPTURE PASSAGE comes from the story of David and Goliath. While the other Israelite troops were too afraid to take up Goliath's challenge to one-on-one combat, David was incensed by his audacity. So when no one else took up his challenge, David decided to do it himself.

Although his brother Eliab was angry with him and Saul was ready to dismiss him, David was confident. He said, "The LORD who rescued me from the claws of the lion and the bear will rescue me from this Philistine!" (1 Samuel 17:37). Saul gave him his own armor, but since David was still a teenager, it hung off him like an oversize jacket.

Saul meant well, of course, but David believed his protection didn't lie in armor. Although he seemed desperately weak—and indeed, he was—David knew where real strength was to be found: in God alone. He knew that in such times of weakness, God's strength really comes into its own. And when David struck down Goliath "with only a sling and a stone" (1 Samuel 17:50), he was proved right! The rest is history.

Feeling weak today? Good! For the weaker you are, the better; because the more aware you are of your weakness, the more God can show his power, just as he promised.

This foolish plan of God is wiser than the wisest of human plans, *and God's weakness is stronger than the greatest of human strength.*

1 CORINTHIANS 1:25

ALYSSUM
Alyssum, whose name means "worth beyond beauty" or "sweetness of soul," belongs to the mustard family and displays small yellow, white, pink, and violet flowers.

Who Speaks

*I listen carefully to what God the LORD is saying,
for he speaks peace to his faithful people.* PSALM 85:8

AS INHERITORS OF GREEK THINKING, Westerners have tended to keep the "spiritual" and the "secular" in separate boxes: God and religion in one box; "the real world" in the other. Because of this, Western Christians have often thought of faith as something entirely otherworldly, having little expectation that God will reach out of his "box" into everyday life. But this isn't the God of the Bible! There God is revealed as fully involved in his world, engaging with his people and constantly speaking to them. Our God is the God who speaks!

To heighten this fact, the Old Testament often contrasts the living God with idols, mocking the fact that "they have mouths but cannot speak, and eyes but cannot see. They have ears but cannot hear, and noses but cannot smell. They have hands but cannot feel, and feet but cannot walk, and throats but cannot make a sound" (Psalm 115:5-7). But this isn't our God!

Our God speaks in so many different ways, as the Bible shows—through visions, dreams, pictures, angels, circum-stances, the Scriptures, and sometimes even an audible voice. This truth is amazing, as Israel's leaders and elders realized when they said, "Today we have seen that God can speak to us humans, and yet we live!" (Deuteronomy 5:24).

God still really wants to speak to people—and that includes you! He is speaking; the challenge is, Are you listening?

What good is an idol carved by man, or a cast image that deceives you? How foolish to trust in your own creation—a god that can't even talk! . . . But the LORD is in his holy Temple.

Let all the earth be silent before him.

HABAKKUK 2:18, 20

CANNA
Cannas boast a tropical appearance with their broad leaves and bright, lily-like blooms that grow atop tall, thick stems.

A TWO-WAY
Conversation

"Come now, let's settle this," says the LORD. ISAIAH 1:18

EVER TRIED TO HAVE a conversation with someone who doesn't listen? All they do is talk. And even if you do get a word in, the conversation quickly comes back to them again. Have you ever wondered if your talks with God might be a bit like that, where you do all the talking and none of the listening?

But if you dig deep into the Bible, you'll discover that some of the best prayers are two-way conversations. One of the longest is in Exodus 3:1–4:17, where God calls Moses to lead Israel out of their slavery in Egypt, and Moses comes up with several excuses for why he is unsuitable. Moses asks, "Who am I to appear before Pharaoh?" and God replies, "I will be with you." Next, Moses asks what he should say if the Israelites wonder who sent him. God answers, "Say this to the people of Israel: I AM has sent me to you."

But Moses protests, "What if they won't believe me or listen to me?" God replies, "What is that in your hand?" and performs three miracles that Moses can repeat to the Israelites to confirm his authority. Then Moses claims he's not a public speaker. But God says, "Who makes a person's mouth? . . . Now go! I will be with you as you speak." What an incredible prayer conversation!

How our own prayers might change if we engaged in two-way conversation—both talking and listening to God until things are clear. Why not try it today—as you walk, as you drive the car, as you stand at the sink. God himself invites you to do it!

What good is an idol carved by man, or a cast image that deceives you? How foolish to trust in your own creation—a god that can't even talk!

HABAKKUK 2:18

TORENIA

Torenias look like trumpeters or choirs in joyful song. Some people see cheery faces in their blooms. They also resemble their cousins, snapdragon and foxglove.

The Faithful God

*Great is his faithfulness; his mercies begin afresh
each morning.* LAMENTATIONS 3:23

"I WON'T BE YOUR FRIEND anymore if you don't do what I want!" We've all probably heard children saying something like this to one of their friends. And come to think of it, we've probably heard adults saying similar things too—though in a far more sophisticated way, of course! Thankfully, God's friendship is completely unconditional. He never manipulates, demands, or sulks if we let him down or won't cooperate. God's friendship is simply there for us—a friendship of *covenant*.

Through his Son, Jesus, God has made a covenant with us—a binding commitment to work out his purposes in us, come what may, and to remain our friend in the process. It is this "come what may" that characterizes his faithfulness. What a wonderful phrase! To think that the God of the universe has promised to be *with* you and *for* you, *come what may*!

You may be wondering, *But how can I be sure?* The answer is clear: Because God has already demonstrated his commitment in sending his Son, Jesus, to die on the cross for our sins. And as the apostle Paul puts it, "Since [God] did not spare even his own Son but gave him up for us all, won't he also give us everything else?" (Romans 8:32).

God is there, and God is faithful—always—and not because of your own faithfulness, but because of what Jesus did. Today, you can be confident of experiencing that faithfulness afresh, whatever your situation.

He is the Rock; his deeds are perfect. Everything he does is just and fair. He is a faithful God who does no wrong;

how just and upright he is!

DEUTERONOMY 32:4

LEADWORT

The leadwort is as unique as its name. It blooms with blue flowers, and eventually its leaves turn red for a show of autumn color.

GOD LOVES
Enthusiasts!

> *They earnestly sought after God, and they found him. And the LORD gave them rest from their enemies on every side.* 2 CHRONICLES 15:15

HAVE YOU NOTICED how easy it is to feel embarrassed by enthusiasts? Whether in the church or the workplace or the stadium, enthusiasts can . . . well, just go over the top, can't they? Of course, the real reason we find enthusiasts hard to cope with at times is because they reveal our own lack of enthusiasm. Perhaps the problem, therefore, is not theirs but ours.

In fact, the Bible shows that God loves enthusiasts! He loves people who seek him eagerly, worship him eagerly, pray eagerly, serve him eagerly, and share about him eagerly; and the Bible often speaks of God's blessing on such enthusiasts, as 2 Chronicles 15:15 shows. Elsewhere we find the Bereans listening "eagerly to Paul's message" (Acts 17:11); the Corinthians being commended for how they "eagerly wait for the return of our Lord Jesus Christ" (1 Corinthians 1:7); and Peter commending leaders for being "eager to serve God" (1 Peter 5:2). In short, eagerness seems to get pretty good press!

Eagerness and enthusiasm should characterize every aspect of our lives—the way we study God's Word; the way we share our faith with those who don't know Jesus yet; the way we pray; the way we engage in worship; the way we give; the way we serve. All should be characterized by passion and enthusiasm.

Why not ask God to search your heart today and show you any areas where you have become passive. Repent of passivity and resolve to be an enthusiast! When you are, there is the promise of great blessing.

You should earnestly desire the most helpful gifts.

1 CORINTHIANS 12:31

CORYDALIS
The herb corydalis, a relative of the poppy, grows diversely in China and is known as a pain reliever in ancient Chinese medicine.

STEPPING OUT
with God

Abraham never wavered in believing God's promise.
In fact, his faith grew stronger, and in this he brought glory
to God. He was fully convinced that God is able
to do whatever he promises.

ROMANS 4:20-21

TRUST IS A RARE COMMODITY these days. Can we trust politicians, the media, our employers, our friends? It can sometimes be hard to know. But one thing that can help us decide is their track record. If they've been trustworthy in the past, it's likely they will be again in the future.

Yet when Abraham first stepped out with God in his walk of faith, he had no track record to go by. Coming from Ur, he would have been a moon worshiper, like everyone else there. But God revealed himself to Abraham, saying, "Leave your native country, your relatives, and your father's family, and go to the land that I will show you" (Genesis 12:1).

There was just one problem—he didn't say which land! It was only when Abraham got there that God said, "This is it!" Abraham had to leave everything—home, family, friends, his old way of life—and step into the unknown by trusting God. But if he hadn't done so, he would never have discovered whether God's promise was true—because faith doesn't drop out of the sky; it grows as we risk stepping out with God.

Through reading the Bible, we can look at God's track record in a way Abraham never could. Let his faithfulness strengthen your resolve to step out with him today into whatever he brings along. Dare to take hold of his promises!

It was by faith that Abraham obeyed

when God called him to leave home and go to another land that God would give him as his inheritance. He went without knowing where he was going.

HEBREWS 11:8

NASTURTIUM
Bright yellow, orange, and red nasturtiums are beautiful to behold and also taste delicious. They're loaded with vitamin C, manganese, iron, flavonoids, and beta-carotene.

Always Rejoice

Always be full of joy in the Lord. I say it again—rejoice! PHILIPPIANS 4:4

IF ANYONE IN THE BIBLE knew how to set his heart on praising God in difficult times, it was the apostle Paul; for he wrote Philippians 4:4 while sitting in jail for his faith. Yet this verse, which encourages other Christians to do the same, has often been misunderstood. Some have interpreted Paul's words as saying, "Praise God for everything, even the bad circumstances in life!" But to insist that's the case is to turn God into a monster who sends awful things our way and expects us to thank him for them. So what did Paul really mean?

His exhortation isn't to rejoice in the circumstances, but to rejoice "in the Lord"—a small but significant difference. God doesn't expect us to praise him *for* everything; but he does want us to praise him *in* everything. Why? Because when our focus is on him and not on our problems, good things start to happen—if not in our situations, then at least in us.

Most of us don't find it easy to praise God in hard times. The truth is, it involves real sacrifice: a sacrifice of our feelings, questions, and doubts. But God always blesses sacrifice!

Today, even—and especially—if you're facing difficult times, set your heart on praising God for who you know him to be: your loving Father who ultimately causes all the events of life to work together for your good and his purpose. And as you do, see how things—and most of all, you!—begin to change.

Let us offer through Jesus a continual sacrifice of praise to God, proclaiming our allegiance to his name. HEBREWS 13:15

WISTERIA

Wisteria often innocently drapes a fence or trellis, attracting many with its intoxicating scent. It's also a dominator that, without pruning, can overtake other plants.

Comparison

Pay careful attention to your own work, for then you will get the satisfaction of a job well done, and you won't need to compare yourself to anyone else. For we are each responsible for our own conduct. GALATIANS 6:4-5

THE WORLD OF ADVERTISING revolves around getting people to compare themselves with others, making them think they would be happier if only they wore the same clothes, used the same lotion, or drove the same car as a famous TV star. The trouble is, this all too easily spills over into our spiritual lives, and we start to make comparisons there, too. Before we know it, we're wondering why God seems to bless everyone else more than us, and soon we feel completely useless or utterly rejected.

When we ask these kinds of questions, however, we're fundamentally challenging God by telling him he doesn't know how to run our lives—though we will, of course, piously sing on Sunday that he knows how to run the world. But those with truly thankful hearts believe that God's purposes are good, gratefully receiving whatever he gives without comparing themselves to others—and trusting him even when things don't work out quite the way they'd hoped.

If you've been comparing yourself to others recently or longing for what they have, just stop! God loves you exactly as you are and is providing for you in exactly the way that is right for you at this time. The only person you should be comparing yourself with is . . . yourself! Seek to be a better Christian than you were this time last week, last month, last year. Only this comparison bears fruit for God!

A peaceful heart leads to a healthy body; jealousy is like cancer in the bones.

PROVERBS 14:30

RHODODENDRON

Rhododendrons love temperate climates without extremes. Of the more than one thousand species, none are indigenous to Africa or South America.

No Hiding Place

"Can anyone hide from me in a secret place? Am I not everywhere in all the heavens and earth?" says the LORD. JEREMIAH 23:24

TRY AS WE MIGHT, we simply can't hide from God—though many of us attempt to, especially when we've messed up in some way. And while that's the very moment we need God, everything within us wants to run and hide, just like Adam and Eve did. When they disobeyed God by eating the forbidden fruit in the Garden of Eden, they foolishly "hid from the LORD God among the trees" (Genesis 3:8).

People have been doing the same ever since—even King David, who tried to cover up his sin after forcing himself upon Bathsheba. When he found out Bathsheba was carrying his child, he recalled her husband, Uriah, from the battlefront in hopes that Uriah would sleep with her. Then it would appear the baby was Uriah's. But despite David's repeated attempts, this was something Uriah wouldn't do while his fellow soldiers were in such danger.

And then David thought he could conceal his wrongdoing by arranging for Uriah's death and quickly marrying Bathsheba. But David still couldn't hide his sin from God, who sent Nathan the prophet to confront him through a parable (2 Samuel 12:1-12). At that moment, David finally realized the solution: Stop running and own up. When he did, the matter was immediately forgiven. He discovered that God will always forgive those who confess their sin.

Acknowledging there is no hiding place from God may seem frightening (and Satan will try to convince you of this), but it's actually freeing! So today, don't run from God; instead, talk to him. After all, he already knows everything—so why keep running?

Nothing in all creation is hidden from God.

Everything is naked and exposed before his eyes, and he is the one to whom we are accountable.

HEBREWS 4:13

TULIP

Tulips are classic spring flowers that were first cultivated in the Ottoman Empire. During Holland's mid-seventeenth century "Tulip Mania," they were used as money.

Comfort Principle

He comforts us in all our troubles so that we can comfort others.
When they are troubled, we will be able to give them the same
comfort God has given us. 2 CORINTHIANS 1:4

THE LAST THING WE NEED when we're struggling is for someone to dispense trite truths without thought or feeling, or glib consolations that "God has it under control." Job had friends like that—and described them as "miserable comforters" (Job 16:2)! What helps us at such times isn't an answer to the problem, but a squeezed hand, a hug, a phone call, a cake . . . reassurances that we're loved by someone who will listen and won't try to "fix" us.

But once we've come through our struggles, we're in a strong place to help others who are going through the same things. That was certainly the apostle Paul's experience. He knew what it was both to be comforted and to comfort, and he saw this as a principle of how God works among his people.

In his second letter to the Corinthians, Paul wrote about a time when he and his companions were in desperate need of comfort: "God, who encourages those who are discouraged, encouraged us by the arrival of Titus. His presence was a joy, but so was the news he brought of the encouragement he received from you" (2 Corinthians 7:6-7). Encouragement was making the rounds!

Whatever your situation, God has comfort that is appropriate to it. He
wants you to dig deeper into him, take hold of his comfort, and then pass
it on. Will you do this today?

May our Lord Jesus Christ himself and God our Father, who loved us and by his grace gave us eternal comfort and a wonderful hope,

comfort you and strengthen you

in every good thing

you do and say.

2 THESSALONIANS 2:16-17

BEGONIA
Begonias are agreeable, easy-to-grow plants that come in a variety of sizes and flower shapes. A little fertilizer boosts proliferous blooms.

Living the Truth

When the Spirit of truth comes, he will guide you into all truth.

JOHN 16:13

"WHAT IS TRUTH?" Pilate asked Jesus (John 18:38). Did he mean "Does truth matter?" or "How can anyone know what truth is anyway?" Whatever he meant, it was the kind of attitude we meet in our modern world, where the idea of absolute truth is rejected and unpopular truths are dismissed as fake news.

In contrast to this, Jesus came into the world not simply *bringing* the truth but *being* the truth. "I *am* . . . the truth," he declared (John 14:6, emphasis added). And the Holy Spirit, whom he promised to send after he ascended to his Father, would continue as "the Spirit of truth." Yet truth isn't just about *right theology;* it's also about *right living.*

Truth is a person, not a concept; so living in truth is about living with the Holy Spirit, who loves truth. We aren't living in the truth if we "stand up for truth"—perhaps defending some doctrine or action—but are arrogant and ungracious in the way we do so. There is also little that rings true if we condemn the sins of others while living in secret sin ourselves.

Do I want to *stand up* for truth? Then I'll look to the Spirit of truth to lead me. Do I want to *live out* the truth? Then I'll obey the Scriptures that the Spirit of truth inspired. Do I want to *grow in* the truth? Then I'll respond in the way the Spirit of truth leads me. For truth is for living, not just for learning.

Today, ask the Holy Spirit to lead you into truth—and then do whatever he tells you.

God is Spirit, so those who worship him must worship in spirit and in truth.

JOHN 4:24

PRIMROSE
Shakespeare mentioned primroses in several plays and sonnets. They blossom in many colors, such as white, yellow, orange, red, blue, pink, and purple.

the Letter

After Hezekiah received the letter from the messengers and read it, he went up to the LORD's Temple and spread it out before the LORD.

ISAIAH 37:14

IT'S EASY TO SAY to someone, "I trust you!"—until we actually need to put that trust into action. That's when we may start to have second thoughts or wonder if we were too quick with our promise. But real trust demands action. And sometimes, God puts us into situations to see whether we really trust *him*.

This was the position King Hezekiah found himself in when he received a threatening letter from Assyrian messengers. Despite King Sennacherib's warning that his army would destroy Jerusalem, Hezekiah didn't panic (though he had plenty of grounds to do so!). Rather, he put his trust into action. He took the letter and "spread it out before the LORD" in the Temple. It was his way of saying, "Do you see this, God? Do you see what these unbelievers are threatening to do?"

After Hezekiah spread out the letter, he "prayed . . . before the LORD" (Isaiah 37:15), proclaiming God's greatness, declaring him to be the God of heaven and earth and describing the letter as an insult. Hezekiah finished with this plea: "O LORD our God, rescue us from his power; then all the kingdoms of the earth will know that you alone, O LORD, are God" (verse 20). Here was trust in action. And God rescued the city!

Is there a circumstance in your life that you need to "spread out" before the LORD today? It's about recognizing you can't deal with this on your own and committing yourself totally to him. When you do, surprising things can happen.

I entrust my spirit into your hand.

Rescue me, LORD, for you are a faithful God. PSALM 31:5

FOXGLOVE
Foxglove is grown commercially to produce the cardiac drug digitalis. However, the raw plant is highly toxic. Ingesting even a small amount is dangerous.

THE ART OF
Remembering

Samuel then took a large stone and placed it between the towns of Mizpah and Jeshanah. He named it Ebenezer (which means "the stone of help"), for he said, "Up to this point the LORD has helped us!" 1 SAMUEL 7:12

WE PROBABLY ALL HAVE TIMES when we're rummaging through our drawers and find something from the past we've completely forgotten about. For a few moments, all the memories come flooding back—before we stuff the object back again to await the next clear-out.

We can be the same way with God sometimes: forgetful of what he's done for us, with too many memories "stuffed in the drawer." That's why Samuel did what he did. God had given Israel a supernatural victory over the Philistines, so Samuel set up a large stone, calling it Ebenezer ("the stone of help") to make sure God's people would never forget this great blessing. Every time they walked past it, they were to think, *Ah yes! God helped us win that victory! He can do it again!*

We, too, need ways of putting "Ebenezers" into our own lives so we don't forget God's blessings—both the "ordinary" ones we so easily take for granted and the "special" ones that changed our lives in some way. Those "Ebenezers" can take so many forms: stopping to give thanks before a meal; posting Bible verses on the fridge; keeping mementos of times when God intervened; pinning up photos of special events and people on our bulletin boards. The list is endless!

Is there an "Ebenezer" that God would have you set up today to help you remember his faithfulness?

Let all that I am praise the LORD; may I never forget

the good things he does for me.

PSALM 103:2

HYACINTH

The hyacinth's fragrance can fill a garden. Its bell-shaped blooms come in a variety of bright colors and are among the first to greet spring.

Our Watchful Guide

The LORD keeps watch over you as you come and go,
both now and forever. PSALM 121:8

HAVE YOU EVER STRUGGLED with the issue of God's guidance, wanting to make certain you're pursuing the right career, buying the right home, taking the right job, marrying the right person? Being sure of his guidance isn't always easy; but the guidance of God becomes clearer and easier the more we get to know the God of guidance. For the more we learn about him and his ways, the more we know instinctively what is right.

Knowing the right thing to do becomes a major issue only if we're uncertain about God or our relationship with him. If we see him as just a celestial career adviser or lifestyle guru, we're missing the point! He's our loving Father who is constantly rooting for us and watching over us. So we don't have to persuade him to guide; he is always there as the watchful Guide.

And this watchful Guide brings his guidance in so many ways: through his Word (the Bible), his people (and the counsel they bring), his gifts (such as wisdom and prophecy), his voice (that quiet inner conviction we can't explain), his hand (as he opens and closes doors). When several of these come into line, that's when it's safest to step out with him.

If you are seeking God's guidance, be encouraged that the watchful Guide is always with you. He has a plan and will lead you into it. But don't pursue the plan; pursue the Guide.

With your unfailing love you lead the people you have redeemed. *In your might, you guide them to your sacred home.*

EXODUS 15:13

LISIANTHUS

The classy lisianthus resembles a rose and blooms in several colors. Both buds and full blossoms are elegant in a garden or vase.

Proof of Change

Salvation has come to this home today, for this man has shown himself to be a true son of Abraham. LUKE 19:9

ZACCHAEUS, ABOUT WHOM Jesus spoke in Luke 19:9, had spent his life as a tax collector and had become very wealthy along the way. The Roman tax system was set up not only to collect money for Rome but also to make fat profits for the tax collectors, who bought the right to raise taxes for a particular region in exchange for a fixed payment. This gave Rome the advantage of getting paid up front, and for tax collectors, it meant Rome's soldiers supported their tax demands on others—including hefty surcharges added for their own profits. Little wonder Zacchaeus was so despised.

But when Zacchaeus brought Jesus to his house after Jesus called him down from the tree that day, his whole life was touched—including his money. Zacchaeus immediately said he would give half his possessions to the poor and repay "four times as much" (Luke 19:8) to those he had cheated. Proof of change indeed!

Genuine salvation will always demonstrate itself through change—especially in how we handle our money. But it will likely manifest in other ways too. For converts in Ephesus, it meant burning their expensive sorcery scrolls (Acts 19:18-20); for Peter and Andrew, it meant giving up their careers (Matthew 4:18-20); and for Lydia, it meant opening up her home to the church in Philippi (Acts 16:13-15, 40). All this showed, just as Zacchaeus himself had experienced, that salvation had come to their homes.

Today, don't walk away from any area where God has been challenging you to change. Whatever the cost, embrace it. It will bring joy to both yourself and others.

If you want to be perfect, go and sell all your possessions and give the money to the poor, and you will have treasure in heaven.

Then come, follow me.

MATTHEW 19:21

NEW ENGLAND ASTER
Late-blooming New England asters provide important autumn nectar for monarch butterflies as they prepare to migrate to Mexico.

Tested

When troubles of any kind come your way, consider it an opportunity for great joy. For you know that when your faith is tested, your endurance has a chance to grow. So let it grow, for when your endurance is fully developed, you will be perfect and complete, needing nothing.

JAMES 1:2-4

IT'S ALWAYS EASIER to see others going through testing than to endure it ourselves—and to stand with them in their difficulties than to stand in our own. But the time inevitably comes when it's our turn to face the challenges and tests of life. And when we do, two promises from God's Word can help us.

The first is that God tests us not because he doesn't love us, but because he does. Trials and tests prove that God is treating us "as his own children" (Hebrews 12:7). God is giving us the opportunity to grow in faith, trust, and character by putting our roots deeper into him.

The second promise is that "God is faithful. He will not allow the temptation [or the test] to be more than you can stand" (1 Corinthians 10:13). Asking Abraham to sacrifice Isaac wasn't the only occasion when God tested Abraham's faith, but it was certainly the most stretching. Yet Abraham was ready because by then he had proved God over the years.

God never gives us burdens beyond what he knows we can carry at the time. So if you're going through difficult times of testing, take these promises to heart. Above all, remember God is with you today in all that you face.

Trials will show that your faith is genuine. It is being tested
as fire tests and purifies gold—

*though your faith is far more
precious than mere gold.*

1 PETER 1:7

CHIVE

Chives carry the notable
fragrance of their onion family,
while purple, spherical blooms
add a hint of whimsy to their
slender stems.

Your Troubles

Around midnight Paul and Silas were praying and singing hymns to God, and the other prisoners were listening. Suddenly, there was a massive earthquake, and the prison was shaken to its foundations. All the doors immediately flew open, and the chains of every prisoner fell off! ACTS 16:25-26

TROUBLE FOLLOWED the apostle Paul wherever he went. He didn't go looking for it; his passionate commitment to sharing the Good News simply got him into it—constantly. For example, in Philippi, he and Silas freed a slave girl from a spirit of fortune-telling; but her owners were livid that their source of income had now dried up. So they stirred up a riot, which resulted in Paul and Silas being flogged and thrown into prison.

In trouble again! But rather than falling into self-pity, Paul and Silas started to praise God. And as they did, an earthquake struck the city, bursting open the jail's doors and breaking the prisoners' shackles. But rather than run (as any normal prisoner would have done!), Paul and Silas saw their newfound freedom as just another opportunity to preach the Good News.

Paul refused to let himself be troubled by "trouble." Rather, when trouble came along, he went on the offensive and troubled the trouble—disturbing it and turning it around for good. And he did this through praise. Praise works—not because of any intrinsic power within itself, but because it sets our hearts on God, who alone can turn our troubles into victory.

Today, if you are facing any kind of trouble, make up your mind to trouble it through praise. It releases God's hand to do amazing things!

You are my hiding place; you protect me from trouble.

You surround me with songs of victory.

PSALM 32:7

SNOWDROP

Snowdrops are charmingly named for their shape and color. They're also among the first to bid farewell to the snow as spring arrives.

All the Time!

I am confident I will see the LORD's goodness while I am here in the land of the living. Wait patiently for the LORD. Be brave and courageous. Yes, wait patiently for the LORD. PSALM 27:13-14

FINDING QUALITY PRODUCTS isn't always easy. You can do all the research you like in order to buy a good car or home appliance, but it still might have hidden faults. And finding really good people can be an even bigger challenge. After all, appearances can be deceptive; and even the best of people can let you down.

But in contrast to all this, one of the Bible's most basic affirmations is that God is good—really good—all the time. There is nothing faulty, deceptive, or unreliable about him. From start to finish, he is good through and through.

His goodness is something the Old Testament prophets often underscored. They stressed that he wasn't like the pagan deities of the surrounding nations, whose character and attitudes were always "changing." Worshipers of those false gods had to take care not to "upset" them in case they became angry. No, the living God is good through and through—day after day, year after year. That's why the psalmist could declare with such confidence, "You are good and do only good" (Psalm 119:68). The psalmist might have had his ups and downs, but at the end of the day, he was confident that God was good and was committed to doing him only good.

God is good—all the time! And God does good—all the time! So affirm—and enjoy—his goodness today.

Let my soul be at rest again,
for the LORD has been good to me.

PSALM 116:7

AMARYLLIS
Bell-shaped and vibrant,
amaryllises resemble lilies.
They bloom indoors during the
winter, and over time, their bulbs
continue to flourish and
produce more stems.

A CALL TO
Compassion

Give generously to the poor, not grudgingly, for the LORD your God will bless you in everything you do. DEUTERONOMY 15:10

WHEN MOSES ASKED to see God's glory, God graciously revealed himself to him on Mount Sinai. And the staggering thing is what God said as he did so: "Yahweh! The LORD! The God of compassion and mercy!" (Exodus 34:6). How incredible that the first thing God wants us to know about him is that he is *compassionate*. It shouldn't surprise us, then, to find that God calls his people to be compassionate too—and promises to bless those who are.

In the Old Testament, the law called God's people to show compassion to those in need, as in Deuteronomy 15:10 above. The prophets challenged those who didn't (Amos 4:1-3; 8:4-10), and Jesus taught his followers, "You must be compassionate, just as your Father is compassionate" (Luke 6:36). When Paul met the church leaders in Jerusalem, the one need that James, Peter, and John emphasized was to "keep on helping the poor," which Paul said he had "always been eager to do" (Galatians 2:10).

Our compassionate God wants compassionate people. And here's the amazing part: Whenever we are compassionate to others, God blesses us. He is more than able to repay us for any kindness we extend to others—though, of course, this shouldn't be our reason for doing so. God wants us to be compassionate as a reflection of his heart, not as a means of squeezing blessings out of him for ourselves.

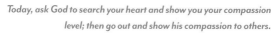

Today, ask God to search your heart and show you your compassion level; then go out and show his compassion to others.

Whoever gives to the poor will lack nothing, but those who close their eyes to poverty will be cursed.

PROVERBS 28:27

IRIS

Irises are among the first spring bloomers, but they can blossom a second time in late summer. The word *iris* means "rainbow."

THE GOD WHO
Gets Involved

[The LORD] was amazed to see that no one intervened to help the oppressed. So he himself stepped in to save them with his strong arm. ISAIAH 59:16

WE LIVE IN A WORLD where people often don't like to get involved—especially if it's going to cost them in some way. But thankfully, God isn't some remote creator who stands far off, unconcerned. Because of his great compassion, he loves to get involved!

The Bible sometimes likens him to a potter carefully shaping clay on his wheel (Isaiah 64:8; Jeremiah 18:1-11). What a powerful picture of how closely God loves to get involved with our lives—pushing his fingers into messy clay to shape it! That should give us great encouragement and security, knowing we're clay in his hands.

But it also means he can do with us as he pleases. His involvement sometimes means squeezing out the lumps or reshaping the clay—and that doesn't feel pleasant! Yet thankfully, he knows what he's doing since he is our loving Father who "causes everything to work together for the good of those who love God" (Romans 8:28).

If you're sensing God's fingers pressing into the clay of your life at this time, don't be fearful. It's just his involvement for your good! Look back and remember the many times he has intervened in the past on your behalf; and as you do, let it help you to look forward in trusting anticipation of his good involvement once again.

Since the world began, no ear has heard
and no eye has seen a God like you,

who works for those who wait for him!

ISAIAH 64:4

DAFFODIL

Warm-weather lovers welcome
the emergence of daffodil leaves,
which signal spring is near. Days
later, cheery yellow trumpet
blooms brighten the dormant
winter landscape.

Wonderful World!

The heavens proclaim the glory of God. The skies display his craftsmanship. Day after day they continue to speak; night after night they make him known. PSALM 19:1-2

TO STAND OUTSIDE and look at the night sky is a wonderful experience. All those stars! And as we keep looking, we just keep seeing more and more. But even those are just a tiny part of what's out there. How vast and splendid God's creation is!

Many of the Psalms reflect this feeling too (Psalms 8, 19, and 104). As the psalmists looked up into the night sky, they were overwhelmed by what they saw. But their wonder didn't stop at the starlit sky; they saw beyond the glory of the stars to the glory of the God who had created them. Such splendor is so obvious, David wrote in Psalm 8:2, that even children can see it and praise God; and their instinctive awe silences those who have lost the ability to wonder at anything.

But this wonderful creation didn't just happen; it was the work of God himself—"the work of [his] fingers" (Psalm 8:3). No matter what your theory is about how creation came into being, it's here because *God* made it. Creation has a Creator.

As you go through your day, make sure you take time to stop and look at the world around you. Enjoy it, delight in it—and remember that the one who made it is with you.

Ever since the world was created, people have seen the earth and sky. Through everything God made, they can clearly see his invisible qualities—his eternal power and divine nature. So they have no excuse for not knowing God.

ROMANS 1:20

HIBISCUS
Big and colorful hibiscus flowers aren't only beautiful; their blooms and leaves can also be brewed for tea and used for medicinal benefits.

to Change

> *True circumcision . . . is a change of heart produced by the Spirit. And a person with a changed heart seeks praise from God, not from people.* ROMANS 2:29

CHANGE. You either love it or you hate it. Some people find it exciting, while others find it more challenging and prefer the steady certainty of routine. But whatever our natural inclinations, change is something that God looks for in us all. For change lies at the heart of the Good News.

The challenge to change was central to Jesus' message. His ministry began with the announcement that God's Kingdom was near. He challenged the people, "Repent of your sins and believe the Good News!" (Mark 1:15). The expression "repent of your sins" is a translation of a Greek word that means "change"—specifically, a change of mind or heart that leads to a change of action.

Repentance isn't just about saying "I'm sorry" but then living as before. True repentance means *saying* sorry and then *living* sorry. It isn't something we do just to become Christians; it's something we continue to do as we live as Christians. From the moment we first believe and repent, we are called to lives of constant change.

How have you been responding to challenges to change recently? Have you been resisting change or embracing it? Remember: Change is what you were called to and what proves you are still following Jesus.

*Prove by the way you live
that you have repented of your sins
and turned to God.* LUKE 3:8

MOONFLOWER
Moonflowers were made for balmy summer evenings, when they open at dusk and waft an enticing fragrance. Heart-shaped leaves surround their purple and white blooms.

Just Stop!

Stop and consider the wonderful miracles of God! JOB 37:14

LIFE IS SO BUSY TODAY. Yes, we have more technology and labor-saving aids than ever before, but we still always seem to have so much to do. And because of that, relationships tend to get pushed aside since relationships demand time.

The story of Martha and Mary reminds us of the importance of stopping and prioritizing relationships. Martha had invited Jesus and his disciples home for a meal, but having invited them, she became increasingly anxious about getting the food ready. Meanwhile, Mary just sat at Jesus' feet, listening to his teaching. We can imagine the thoughts going on in Martha's head: *Doesn't that girl know how much there is to be done? Why doesn't she get herself into the kitchen and help out?!*

Martha eventually became so annoyed that she said, "Lord, doesn't it seem unfair to you that my sister just sits here while I do all the work? Tell her to come and help me" (Luke 10:40). But Jesus wouldn't play her game. "My dear Martha," he replied, "you are worried and upset over all these details! There is only one thing worth being concerned about. Mary has discovered it, and it will not be taken away from her" (verses 41-42).

Martha needed to learn how to prioritize relationship. Relationship takes time, and that means knowing how to stop; for when we stop, we're giving God an opportunity to refocus our hearts on him as our Father and on others as those made in his image.

What about you? Are you like Mary, who stopped, or like Martha, who was too busy to stop—too busy for relationship? What is your "one thing worth being concerned about"?

Be still, and know that I am God!

PSALM 46:10

GERANIUM

Popular warm-weather outdoor plants, colorful geraniums can bloom inside all year with enough light. Properly wintered plants can also bloom outside again in spring.

THE GOD
Who Hears

He will be gracious if you ask for help. He will surely respond to the sound of your cries. ISAIAH 30:19

BEING HARD OF HEARING is a real hindrance, as anyone who is getting older and starting to lose their hearing can testify. Things get missed or misunderstood, and frustrations can soon arise. But thankfully, we have a God who isn't deaf or hard of hearing. He is the God who hears.

Isaiah says in the Scripture above that God really does hear when we call to him, and the rest of the Bible affirms this too. An angel told Hagar, the mother of Abram's first son, to name him Ishmael, meaning "God hears" (Genesis 16:11). And David said in Psalm 40:1, "I waited patiently for the LORD to help me, and he turned to me and heard my cry." The testimony of all these, and countless others, is that our God is a God who hears.

In fact, *not* hearing was a mark of idols and the false gods they represented. That's why Elijah taunted Baal's prophets when Baal didn't answer them. "'You'll have to shout louder,' [Elijah] scoffed, 'for surely he is a god! Perhaps he is daydreaming . . . or is asleep and needs to be wakened!'" Despite their frantic efforts, "still there was no sound, no reply, no response" (1 Kings 18:27, 29).

The one true God isn't like this. He always hears! He may not answer immediately, or even in the way we would like; but he always hears and always acts, and it is always good when he does. So today, don't doubt that God hears—and that he hears you.

We are confident that he hears us whenever we ask for anything that pleases him.

1 JOHN 5:14

MAGNOLIA
The magnolia is the official state flower of Mississippi and Louisiana. Regal blooms and glossy leaves make magnolia trees easy to recognize.

the Light

Once you were full of darkness, but now you have light from the Lord. So live as people of light! EPHESIANS 5:8

LIFT UP A ROCK and you will often see little creatures quickly scurrying away, eager to escape the light and find some dark corner again. Some people are like that too. They hate the light—the light of truth, integrity, and honesty—and prefer the darkness of lies, deceit, and cover-up. The Bible says such things are the very opposite of God's nature; and because he hates them, we should hate them too.

But sometimes we live in semidarkness and try to convince ourselves it is light. That's what Ananias and Sapphira did when they claimed to donate the proceeds of a property sale to the church in Jerusalem but had secretly kept much of it back. They put on a mask of generosity when really, they cared only for their reputation. After Peter said they had lied to the Holy Spirit and deceived the church, they dropped down dead (Acts 5:1-11). A sober lesson that darkness isn't our friend.

God wants us to live in the light, not in darkness or even half-light. Sometimes we fear bringing certain matters into the light for fear of what God might say. But he knows all about them anyway! The simple solution is to bring everything—even our sin—into the light; for we have the assurance that when we do, there is always forgiveness and blessing (1 John 1:8-9).

If you've been keeping something in the dark, resolve to stop doing so.
Love the light—and you will find the way out!

We are lying if we say we have fellowship with God but go on living
in spiritual darkness; we are not practicing the truth.

1 JOHN 1:6

IMPATIENS WALLERIANA
When an impatiens walleriana
seedpod ripens, a gentle touch
can burst it open and scatter
the seeds. This prolific
bloomer is nicknamed
"Busy Lizzie."

the Power

You will receive power when the Holy Spirit comes upon you.
And you will be my witnesses, telling people about me everywhere—
in Jerusalem, throughout Judea, in Samaria, and to the ends
of the earth. ACTS 1:7-8

A PERSON'S FINAL WORDS always have special significance—whether those of a politician leaving office or a loved one slipping from this world. Jesus' final words, recorded in Acts 1:8, must have powerfully engraved themselves on the disciples' minds for the rest of their lives. They weren't simply words, but words that became reality when the promised Holy Spirit was given at Pentecost. And the Spirit came to them not just as power without a person or a person without power; both the person *and* the power came!

It's important to remember this link between the person and the power. God's power isn't just some "thing" to be used, as a man named Simon discovered. When he saw Peter and John praying for believers to be filled with the Spirit, he wanted "it." But what he had witnessed wasn't an "it" but a "him," for God's power comes as a person. So Peter replied to Simon, "May your money be destroyed with you for thinking God's gift can be bought! You can have no part in this, for your heart is not right with God" (Acts 8:20-21).

It's sometimes easy to forget that the Holy Spirit is a person—perhaps because of the images used to represent him, like wind, fire, and water. But these describe what the Spirit has come to do (empower, purify, cleanse) rather than who he is—the person of God among us.

Don't go looking for the power of God; look for the person of God! When you do, he will come—just as Jesus promised!

I will ask the Father, and he will give you another Advocate, who will never leave you. He is the Holy Spirit, who leads into all truth.

JOHN 14:9, 16-17

ANGELICA

Angelica is an herb long used as seasoning, medicine, and tea. Its umbrella-shaped clusters of flowers bloom the second year after planting.

THE IMPORTANCE OF
the Heart

The LORD says, "Turn to me now, while there is time. Give me your hearts. Come with fasting, weeping, and mourning. Don't tear your clothing in your grief, but tear your hearts instead." JOEL 2:12-13

TRY TO IMAGINE Washington, DC, without the White House; or Paris without the Eiffel Tower; or Sydney without the Opera House. Those cities just wouldn't be the same, would they? Or imagine a car without its engine and a TV without its screen. There are some things in life which, if you take away their key parts, can't function as they were intended.

And the same is true in our relationship with God: Take "the heart" out of it, and all we're left with is empty religion. Our hearts play such an important role in our lives that God tells us to pay particular attention to them when we come to him; for if our hearts aren't right—trusting, tender, honest, open, teachable—then practices like worship and prayer become meaningless rituals.

This is also why, again and again in the Bible, we find God calling his people to examine their hearts. Though King Saul hadn't carried out all God had commanded him when the Israelites attacked the Amalekites, he thought the prophet Samuel would be pleased he planned to offer sacrifices to the LORD. After all, it showed he wanted God's blessing, didn't it? But Samuel saw a complete lack of heart in Saul's actions. Samuel asked Saul, "What is more pleasing to the LORD: your burnt offerings and sacrifices or your obedience to his voice? Listen! Obedience is better than sacrifice, and submission is better than offering the fat of rams" (1 Samuel 15:22).

God is still looking for one thing from us: our hearts. Prayer, worship, service—all these are secondary. Will we have the courage to examine our hearts and give them fully to God again today?

Search me, O God, and know my heart. PSALM 139:23

ROSE
Roses are beloved special-occasion flowers and bloom in many varieties and colors. Whether one smells as sweet as another is a matter of personal preference.

IMAGE CREDITS